MINORITY RIGHTS IN EUROPE

Hugh Miall

Editor

PUBLISHED IN NORTH AMERICA FOR

THE ROYAL INSTITUTE OF INTERNATIONAL AFFAIRS

COUNCIL ON FOREIGN RELATIONS PRESS
• NEW YORK •

Chatham House Papers

The Royal Institute of International Affairs, at Chatham House in London, has provided an impartial forum for discussion and debate on current international issues for 70 years. Its resident research fellows, specialized information resources, and range of publications, conferences, and meetings span the fields of international politics, economics, and security. The Institute is independent of government.

Chatham House Papers are short monographs on current policy problems which have been commissioned by the RIIA. In preparing the papers, authors are advised by a study group of experts convened by the RIIA, and publication of a paper indicates that the Institute regards it as an authoritative contribution to the public debate. The Institute does not, however, hold opinions of its own; the views expressed in this publication are the responsibility of the author.

Library of Congress Cataloging-in-Publication Data

    Minority rights in Europe : prospects for a transnational regime /
      edited by Hugh Miall .
          p.   cm.
      Originally published : Pinter, 1994.
      Includes bibliographical references.
      ISBN 0-87609-172-9 : $14.95
      1. Human rights–Europe.   2. Minorities–Legal status, laws, etc–
    Europe.   I. Miall , Hugh.
    JC599.E9M56   1994
    323' . 094' 09049–dc20   94-43273
                                    CIP

94 95 96 97 98   PB   10   9   8   7   6   5   4   3   2   1

CONTENTS

List of contributors / vi
Acknowledgments /vii

1 Introduction /1
Hugh Miall

2 Sovereignty and self-determination in the new Europe/7
James Mayall

3 International and European standards on minority rights / 14
Patrick Thornberry

4 Northern Ireland /22
Tom Hadden

5 South Tyrol /46
Antony Alcock

6 The former Yugoslavia /56
Zoran Pajic

7 The rest of the Balkans /66
Hugh Poulton

8 The role of the Council of Europe /87
Klaus Schumann

9 The role of the CSCE /99
Richard Dalton

10 Conclusions /112
Hugh Miall

CONTRIBUTORS

Professor Antony Alcock, Department of European Studies and
Modern Languages, University of Ulster

Richard Dalton, former Head of the CSCE Unit, Foreign and Common-
wealth Office, now Consul-General in Jerusalem

Professor Tom Hadden, Law Department, Queen's University, Belfast

Professor James Mayall, Department of International Relations,
London School of Economics

Dr Hugh Miall, Research Fellow, European Programme, Royal Institute
of International Affairs

Professor Zoran Pajic, formerly Professor of Law at Sarajevo University; Research Centre for Human Rights, School of Law, University
of Essex

Hugh Poulton, author and consultant to the Minority Rights Group,
London

Klaus Schumann, Deputy Political Director and Head of External
Relations, Council of Europe

Dr Patrick Thornberry, Senior Lecturer in Law, Keele University and
Director, Keele University Centre for Minority Rights Research

ACKNOWLEDGMENTS

This paper is the product of a project on minority rights in Europe conducted by the European Programme of the Royal Institute of International Affairs.

We are especially grateful to the contributors who presented drafts of their papers at a Round Table at Chatham House in March 1993 and subsequently revised them for this publication. We also thank all those who participated in the Round Table. I would like to acknowledge the contributions made by Helen Wallace, who initiated the project, Susie Symes, who managed it, Yoram Tzabar, who administered it, Anita Horwich, who was the rapporteur for the Round Table, Margaret May, who edited the final text, and Hannah Doe, who handled the production.

March 1994   Hugh Miall

1

INTRODUCTION

HUGH MIALL

The end of the Cold War has brought the problems of minorities in Europe into sharp prominence. The dissolution of the Soviet empire, followed by the break-up of the Soviet Union, Yugoslavia and Czechoslovakia, resulted in a central and eastern Europe of 28 states. Of these, only six are nationally homogeneous (Albania, Armenia, the Czech Republic, Hungary, Poland and Slovenia); all the others have national minorities comprising over 10 per cent of the population. 'New' minorities have appeared (such as the Russians outside Russia and the Serbs outside Serbia), to add to 'older' minorities (such as the Hungarians outside Hungary). The end of the Cold War has also brought drastic changes in the situation of existing minorities (such as the Albanians outside Albania). The rights and obligations of minorities have become an acute question for minority peoples, for the states in which they dwell and for the European order generally. In particular, the rise of nationalism has brought the issue of minority rights to the top of the European agenda.

It is not surprising that nationalism has found a fertile breeding-ground in the particular circumstances of the post-communist transition. It affects minorities in two ways. First, there has been a strong tendency to consolidate the state by appealing to the nationalism of the majority people: most west European states, after all, are based on a similar alliance between the state and the majority nation. The appeal to ethnic nationalism, however, threatens to exclude minorities and encourages counter-nationalism. Secondly, demands for self-determination may lead minorities to attempt to secede from the host state and create a state of their own. The potential for conflict is apparent when those in power

1

perceive minorities as unreliable and when minorities have no confidence that states will respect their needs for identity and security.

The salience of the minority problem in eastern Europe should not obscure the persistent difficulties west European societies have experienced in managing their own minorities. Some of the more severe conflicts are now in the past, but others (notably in Northern Ireland) testify to the failure to integrate different national, religious or linguistic communities within a single state. This is not to mention the related issue of extra-European minorities in western Europe, which this study does not attempt to cover.

Establishing minority rights – that is, the rights of minorities to receive equal treatment, to practise their culture, religion and language, and to participate fully in the political and economic life of the state – appears to be one of the more promising approaches to this problem. It avoids the extremes of secession and assimilation, and offers a way forward which is compatible with civic, democratic pluralism. But when democracy is itself absent or weak, and when minority issues deeply divide societies, how can minority rights be effectively established, and how can the international community take useful measures to encourage their implementation?

The problems over minorities which have arisen in the wake of the dissolution of the Soviet empire mirror those which followed the collapse of the Russian, Austro-Hungarian and Ottoman empires after the First World War. At that time the efforts of the peacemakers reflected an uneasy mixture of principle and pragmatism. On the one hand, the peacemakers used the principle of self-determination to establish a large number of small new states in eastern Europe. On the other, they adjusted borders in accordance with the power of states and the interests of the Great Powers. The victors intended to weaken Germany and they placed German-speaking minorities under the rule of weak central and east European states. This was eventually to undermine the international order. The peacemakers' attempts to enshrine protection for minorities in the Paris treaties and in the League of Nations system were not without significant successes: the settlement of the Åland Islands dispute in 1920 and 1922 was notable, and some of the new states, such as Estonia, included exemplary protection for minorities in their constitutions. Nevertheless, the system foundered when the Paris treaties came under attack and the democratic order in eastern Europe buckled under the pressures of consolidating the new states. The League of Nations minorities regime could not work in the absence of both democratic systems and the

international will (and means) to protect beleaguered minorities in other states.

A transnational regime for minority rights does exist in the 1990s, but it is still relatively weak. It consists of the protections offered under international law and international conventions such as the European Convention on Political Rights, and the political commitments entered into by member states of the Conference on Security and Cooperation in Europe (CSCE). Together these constitute a code of good practice. States are encouraged to comply by making observance of CSCE commitments a condition of participation in European institutions. CSCE member states have accepted a mutual right of monitoring compliance with these standards, and the CSCE is entitled to send fact-finding and preventive diplomacy missions to their territories. However, there is no formal system for imposing sanctions on member states which breach these standards, unless the international community decides to use economic or military sanctions through the UN.

The aim of this volume is to assess the nature of this regime, to consider how it works with reference to specific cases in western and eastern Europe, and to explore the possibilities for improvement.

Chapters 2 and 3 address minority rights from the point of view of the international political order and the international legal system. In Chapter 2, *James Mayall* discusses the clash between sovereignty and self-determination in the new international system after the Cold War, drawing parallels with the situation after the First World War and with periods of decolonization. He argues that elements of a transnational regime for protecting minorities have come into existence in Europe, but cautions that their distinctiveness from other parts of the world, in terms of capacity to protect, should not be exaggerated. He explores three proposals which could offer minorities more assurance that their interests would be protected: the development of an additional layer of governance at the European level, linked to stronger regions; a system of multilateral surveillance, to monitor abuses; and an international capability to intervene to prevent massive abuses of human rights.

In Chapter 3, *Patrick Thornberry* discusses the present legal status of minority rights. It was not until 1966 that the UN General Assembly adopted any legal provision specifically dealing with minority rights, in Article 27 of the International Covenant on Civil and Political Rights. Its cautious and limited provisions remained the main measure of international law in this area until 1992, when the UN General Assembly adopted the 'Declaration on the Rights of Persons belonging to National

or Ethnic, Religious and Linguistic Minorities'. This mandates states to protect minorities and gives minorities rights to participate in decisions affecting them at national and regional levels. It also introduces obligations on states to promote education in the mother-tongue and knowledge of minority cultures. Reciprocally, it encourages minorities to understand the states in which they find themselves. The rights remain limited to 'persons belonging to national minorities' (although they can be exercised in community with others of the same group) and the document eschews any attempt to define what a minority is (a stumbling-block of previous legislation). Patrick Thornberry concludes with a set of general observations suggesting a framework for further legislation in this area. He stresses that the core of minority rights is the right to existence and identity; that non-discrimination is only a first step towards minority protection; and that while minorities do not have a right to self-determination (that right is vested in *peoples*), they should be able to participate in the self-determination process.

The next four chapters assess minority rights in practice in selected societies in western and eastern Europe. Chapters 4 and 5 examine Northern Ireland and South Tyrol. They explore, first, the extent to which 'the European process' in western Europe has affected or could affect these situations; and, second, whether there are lessons for other parts of Europe.

In Chapter 4 *Tom Hadden* analyses the appeals that have been made to individual and minority rights at different stages of the Northern Ireland conflict. He charts the swing of the pendulum between individual and collective rights, starting from conflicting claims for self-determination, becoming a struggle for individual human rights at the time of the civil rights movement, and later developing into demands for recognition of the right to identity and existence of the two communities. He points out that to stress minority rights may emphasize the divisions in communities and under-represent individuals and households who do not wish to be 'counted' on either side. He argues against communal separation, under which each community might become more responsible for its own affairs, and in favour of a mingling of communities with equal rights of participation for all. Responsibility for a peaceful settlement rests first with the parties in Northern Ireland themselves, and secondly with the British and Irish governments; the role of European institutions in reaching a settlement is limited. He argues, however, that in the context of a settlement the Council of Europe and the CSCE could both have a useful role, especially in building confidence and adjudicating over rights.

South Tyrol, the subject of Chapter 5, is often taken as an exemplary case of minority protection. The German-speaking minority and the Italian state resolved their conflict, largely peacefully, through the granting of autonomy and cultural rights. In analysing the lessons, however, *Antony Alcock* points out some special features of the South Tyrol case. First, it took over forty years to reach the final settlement. Second, the South Tyrolese, in exercising their rights as a separate community, moved towards a system of separate development which entrenches minority privileges – to such an extent that the implementation of the four freedoms of the European Single Market (movement of capital, goods, services and people) may threaten their status. What the South Tyrol case does clearly show, Alcock concludes, is the need for continuous dialogue and adjustment between minority and majority communities in defining their relationship as circumstances change.

Chapters 6 and 7 deal with cases in southeastern Europe where the treatment of minorities has become a source of potential or actual conflict. The former Yugoslavia, and especially Bosnia-Herzegovina, is the extreme case. *Zoran Pajic* argues in Chapter 6 that minority rights can scarcely apply in a society in which human rights do not exist or are subject to massive abuse. Nationalism, he argues, is 'another form of totalitarianism', a reflection of the undemocratic and authoritarian system which has developed in post-communist Yugoslavia. The creators of the new states have associated their identity closely with the dominant nation, leaving no space for those of mixed backgrounds or for those who refuse to accept an ethnic classification. Until the rights of the individual are honoured, there is little hope for establishing rights for minorities.

Hugh Poulton makes a similar point in Chapter 7, in his survey of the minority situations in Albania, Bulgaria, Greece, Kosovo and Macedonia. What is needed, he points out, is protection against arbitrary rule, through independent and democratic institutions: international monitoring missions and the like are only a partial and temporary substitute for this. Against the historical background of large-scale population transfers in the interwar period and denial of minorities' national aspirations during the communist period, this chapter assesses the current situations in the southern Balkans. It argues that the West could do more to assist minorities through a more discriminating distribution of support and censure: in short, by a form of conditionality based on the observance of minority rights.

The role of European institutions forms the subject of the next two chapters. In Chapter 8 *Klaus Schumann* reviews the work of the Council

of Europe, at both the legal and the practical levels. In its legal work, the Council of Europe contributes to a European regime for human rights, particularly through the European Convention on Human Rights, which enables states party to the convention, as well as individuals and organizations, to appeal against violations to the European Commission of Human Rights. The rapid growth of membership of the Council of Europe has extended this regime into eastern Europe, and proposals have been made to extend it on a transitional basis to non-member states, specifically for Bosnia-Herzegovina in the event of a new constitutional settlement. The Council of Europe's pilot projects and confidence-building measures offer a 'bottom-up' approach to the development of trust between minority and majority communities, which has a vital part to play in easing potential tensions. Klaus Schumann discusses some examples of transnational initiatives that the Council of Europe has taken in this direction, such as support for the Carpathian Euroregion, for the independent radio station in Istria and for the reduction of prejudice through history-teaching projects.

Richard Dalton considers the role of the CSCE in Chapter 9. The CSCE has developed a responsibility for minorities throughout Europe, including the whole territory of the former Soviet Union, as a result of its concern with both the 'human dimension' and security aspects. As an intergovernmental organization operating by consensus, the CSCE has had to develop political commitments that take into account the views of states which deny that they have minorities, and of states which perceive their minorities as an active security threat. Despite these constraints, the CSCE has developed an extensive set of standards, together with four means of implementing them. It has been unable to redress the flagrant violation of human rights in civil conflicts that have already broken out, as in the former Yugoslavia. However, it has shown initiative in preventive diplomacy. The creation of the High Commissioner on National Minorities is one of the CSCE's most significant innovations. The High Commissioner contributed to a significant easing of inter-communal tensions in Estonia in 1993.

Chapter 10 draws together conclusions and policy implications. Minority protection should be improved through further development of standards, better domestic implementation of international commitments, and stronger transnational measures to encourage good practice. However, this is contingent on broader progress towards democratization and observance of human rights.

2

SOVEREIGNTY AND SELF-DETERMINATION IN THE NEW EUROPE

JAMES MAYALL

The twentieth century has not been kind to minorities. After 1918 the nation finally inherited the state (at least in theory) but minority groups trapped within these new national states were left out in the cold. However, with the end of the Cold War and the collapse of communism the protection of minority rights has risen to the top of the political agenda for the first time since 1945.

The present situation has much in common with previous periods of decolonization and state-creation. As with the withdrawal of British and French imperial power from Asia and Africa, the end of the Soviet empire has been accompanied by a reassertion of national aspirations and also national animosities. The similarities do not stop there. Then, as now, optimists hoped that decolonization would usher in a new democratic order; pessimists feared that order would be overwhelmed by the forces of anarchy. The problem is that it is not clear whether democracy and nationalism are compatible or antithetical ways of grounding a political community. Some, like Enoch Powell, believe that a nation is a necessary precondition of democracy, since only where a people share an underlying sense of community and values will the minority be prepared to acquiesce in rule by the majority. Others, like Lord Acton in the nineteenth century or Sir Ralf Dahrendorf in the twentieth, saw the ethnic claims of nationalists, whether they belong to the majority or the minority community, as undermining the most basic principles of civil society and democratic government. Either way, unless minorities are prepared to view themselves primarily as citizens rather than as members of an ethnic group, the potential for civil conflict will always be present.

Towards the end of *The Anarchical Society*,[1] one of the most

influential contemporary texts on international relations, Hedley Bull introduced the idea of a 'new medievalism' to suggest the possibility of a different world order from the one which he described in the 1970s. Very broadly, he envisaged circumstances under which the jurisdictional monopoly of the sovereign state would have been broken. States would no doubt survive, but new overlapping and/or competitive forms of jurisdiction would have developed alongside them. Some such idea – suggestive rather than very clear – is one to which minority leaders might be expected to be attracted, if a way forward from their present unenviable plight is to be found. The concept might also be expected to have some resonance in a part of the world which has already devised the hybrid legal and political forms of the European Union, the European Convention of Human Rights, with its optional protocol,* the CSCE, the Council of Europe and other institutions which blur traditional distinctions between domestic and foreign policy.

There is a case, in other words, for holding that Europeans have already begun to fashion a new regional order in which minority protection could have a place, despite the reluctance of governments to surrender their sovereignty in any formal way. But although the European experience may be different from that of other parts of the world, this difference should not be exaggerated. Indeed, the European response to the Bosnian crisis suggests that, in the limiting case, European governments and institutions are no more capable of protecting threatened minorities than those in any other continent. What, then, are the prospects for developing a European transnational regime for minority protection? Before we attempt to answer this question by examining individual cases and the institutional response to the challenge of minority protection, it may be useful, or at least salutary, to ask why minority protection in general has proved such an intractable problem for international society.

Self-determination

The idea of national self-determination was championed by European liberals from the French Revolution onwards, but it was only with the defeat of the Romanov, Ottoman, Hohenzollern and Habsburg dynasties that a principle of popular sovereignty was substituted for prescriptive right as the legal basis of the international order.

This substitution had disturbing implications for the national, as well

---

* See p. 92.

as the dynastic, empires. The French and the British discovered at the Paris Peace Conference in 1919–20 that while it was possible to oppose the principle of national self-determination in particular cases and on pragmatic grounds – in Ireland, India or Alsace – they had no alternative principle to put in its place. From the point of view of national minorities, however, this was a hollow victory. It proved notoriously impossible to redraw the European political map without creating politically marginalized and often disenfranchised minorities in virtually every state.

Woodrow Wilson had originally conceived Article 10 of the League Covenant in a way which would qualify the permanent freehold of the European successor states. He envisaged circumstances arising, either as the result of demographic change or as a consequence of a major shift in public opinion, which would justify a change in territorial boundaries. This idea was so radical that it was opposed even by his own delegation and would certainly have been strongly resisted by the other major powers at the Peace Conference. The draft was quickly forgotten and the final version of the Article asserted the primacy of territorial integrity, although an attempt was made to soften the impact of this major concession to the sovereignty principle by including a system of minority guarantees.

The League's experience with minority protection has generally been judged a failure. Moreover the concept of minority rights fell into disrepute after Hitler had invoked it as a justification for his expansion into central and eastern Europe. Consequently it was abandoned in the UN Charter of 1945, which instead pledged governments to uphold individual rights. From a minority rights perspective, the Charter thus represents a retreat from the legal position, if not the practical one, agreed after 1918. Under the Charter, the principle of state sovereignty is reaffirmed as the basis of international order, but this is combined with the assertion of inalienable human rights. These were separately codified in the Universal Declaration of Human Rights, including the right of all peoples to self-determination.

So much for the formal position. Who in practice would be able to exercise the right? In Europe, the understandings reached at Yalta in 1945 effectively stopped the question being put to the test. The Cold War subsequently froze the political map, incidentally bequeathing to the continent the most stable borders it has enjoyed since the French Revolution. Simply put, self-determination was not a real issue between 1945 and 1989. States were sovereign, or if they were not, there was nothing that could be done about it. As for self-determination, it was implicitly assumed that the peoples of a state had exercised their right at some point in the past.

Outside Europe, national self-determination came to be understood as synonymous with decolonization by the European imperial powers, combined with a reaffirmation of the principle of territorial integrity within the boundaries inherited from these powers. Indeed, over the past forty years, there has been a rare international consensus across both the east/west and the north/south divides that no secessionist right of self-determination should be recognized. Under this formula, states were protected by Article 2(7) of the UN Charter from interference in their internal affairs, including interference on behalf of oppressed minorities.

From a contemporary perspective, it may seem that many of the constraints which currently hinder the effective protection of minorities can be traced to this postwar settlement. It may be worth stressing that the conventional interpretation of self-determination nonetheless has three strong supports, apart from any appeal to cynical self-interest.

The first is practical. The ambiguity of the principle of national self-determination is notorious. Sir Ivor Jennings summed it up in 1956 in a famous remark concerning the UN debates on decolonization: 'On the surface it seemed reasonable: let the People decide. It was in fact ridiculous because the People cannot decide until someone decides who are the People.' Tying self-determination to an existing administrative unit at least has the merit of overcoming this difficulty.

The second justification is philosophical. Its most famous exponent was Abraham Lincoln, who defended the idea of democratic order against the inevitable anarchy which he believed would flow from accepting a right of secession. In his view, in a free society the only way in which a minority could exercise its right of self-determination was by mobilizing public opinion. If successful, in time, and through democratic elections, the minority would become the majority.

The third justification for the conventional interpretation is diplomatic. Statesmen in general fear opening a Pandora's box of secessionist and irredentist claims by conceding the legitimacy of a particular case. Western politicians were extremely reluctant publicly to endorse the break-up of the Soviet Union, even including the secession of the Baltic republics whose incorporation in the USSR they had never recognized. Similarly, they persisted in supporting the maintenance of the Yugoslav Federation long after it had become clear that the state had already disintegrated in the face of a vicious inter-ethnic civil conflict. On several occasions the British Foreign Secretary, Douglas Hurd, urged the Yugoslav leaders to follow the example of the Africans, who had constructed the Organization of African Unity on the basis of respect for colonial

boundaries. Given the enormous human cost of this achievement, it was a strange analogy to choose, but in view of recent events in Bosnia, the diplomatic logic cannot be lightly dismissed.

The conventional interpretation has three obvious weaknesses which mirror these advantages. First, by confining the principle to decolonization, an open invitation was extended to secessionists and irredentists to challenge the basis of international order whenever opportunity offered. International law does not acknowledge a right of minority secession, but since minorities believe, rightly or wrongly, that they have been denied a fundamental human right, they are likely to view the existing legal regime with contempt.

Second, in deeply divided societies, particularly where there are no entrenched democratic traditions, the introduction of a democratic constitution without special provisions for minority protection makes the problem worse rather than better. This is because, as John Stuart Mill was probably the first to point out, where two politically self-conscious national communities share the same polity, the stronger will be tempted to capture the state by democratic means, and then to discriminate against the weaker minority community. Similar considerations influenced Jinnah in his campaign for Indian partition. He argued that the divisions between Hindus and Muslims were so deep that there was no chance of Muslims ever being properly represented in a single democratic Indian state. In a kind of mirror image of these arguments, opponents of the Maastricht Treaty insist that west European democracies are likely to be undermined by over-liberal policies on mobility and immigration.

Third, under the conventional interpretation which equates state with nation, the international community is inhibited from intervening against governments that engage in the systematic abuse of the human rights of sections of their own population. Under Chapter 7 of the Charter, such intervention is permitted only to repel aggression across international frontiers. Not only is there no right of minority secession, there is also no right of humanitarian intervention.

There seems little likelihood that any formal derogation from the principle of state sovereignty will be negotiated in the foreseeable future. Indeed, any attempt to introduce fundamental changes in the Charter would almost certainly be vetoed by China and opposed by many Third World countries. Moreover, the fact that neither the European powers nor the wider international community have been able to prevent ethnic cleansing in Bosnia and parts of the former Soviet Union on a scale not experienced since the 1940s makes it difficult to be confident that legal

guarantees alone will be any more effective than in the past.

On the other hand, the creation of safe havens for Iraqi Kurds and Shi'ites after Operation Desert Storm, the humanitarian interventions in Somalia and the former Yugoslavia, and the development within the CSCE of an early-warning mechanism designed to alert European countries to minority problems before they deteriorate into open conflict, all suggest that the international environment is now more amenable to political initiatives for minority protection than during the Cold War.

A new transnational regime?

What, then, are the political prerequisites of a new transnational regime in which national minorities would have some measure of confidence that their interests and rights will be protected? The most important prerequisite will be flexibility, a willingness to differentiate between cases and needs, since neither states nor the minorities within them are all in the same situation. Beyond this there are three possibilities which deserve further consideration.

The first might be called the Maastricht option. A form of European unification in which some powers are progressively transferred to the centre while others are devolved to the regions could possibly provide a way by which minorities could gain autonomy without opting out of either the state or the open economy. It is notable that most ethnically based regional parties in western Europe are enthusiastic supporters of European integration, although at present their enthusiasm tends to get stuck at the level of generalities. There seems no reason in principle why the Committee of Regions provided for under the Maastricht Treaty should not in time develop mechanisms to support minority identities as well as economic development. The problem is that the most threatened minorities in contemporary Europe are in countries whose accession to the European Union is not likely to be on the political agenda in the foreseeable future.

A second possibility is suggested by analogy with the few peaceful secessions that have occurred during the twentieth century, such as Sweden and Norway in 1905, Britain and the Irish Free State in 1922, and, most recently, Czechoslovakia. In these cases it is clear that the political elites, despite their conflicts over identity, nonetheless shared fundamental political values which in the end made peaceful separation possible. Where such residual common values can be identified, it may be possible to reinforce systems of power-sharing – it would not be

necessary in all cases to opt for secession – by a system of multilateral surveillance. In economic affairs, countries have gradually come to accept that their economic policies are the legitimate interest of their trading partners, and it is conceivable that through the CSCE and the Council of Europe they might similarly come to regard the protection of minorities as a joint concern.

The pursuit of multilateral surveillance is like the debate about preventive medicine in many Western countries. It is an admirable goal for a reformed international society, but it will not be achieved overnight. In the meantime, as with any disease, there is a real need for an improved capacity for diagnosis and dealing with the symptoms. In the present circumstances, when there is a high probability of a succession of 'post-colonial' crises, it would be folly to concentrate exclusively on long-run planning. Many of the worst threats to minorities that have arisen since 1989 fall into this category. In such crises proposals for consociational democracy or other forms of power-sharing are sadly academic. What is needed is a strengthened international capability for rapid and politically robust intervention to prevent the massive abuse of human rights.

With hindsight it seems clear that the Bosnian disaster could have been averted only by stationing substantial forces on the ground prior to recognition. The fact that this strategy was followed in Macedonia, although admittedly on a much more modest scale than would have been necessary to secure Bosnia, provides some basis for hope.

Notes
1 Hedley Bull, *The Anarchical Society: A Study of Order in World Politics* (London: Macmillan, 1977).

3

INTERNATIONAL AND EUROPEAN STANDARDS ON MINORITY RIGHTS

PATRICK THORNBERRY

Introduction

There is a widespread feeling in the international community that the age of standard-setting in human rights is over. But this can never be completely the case. New issues and categories of human deprivation constantly impress themselves on us and demand remedial action in the form of more specific international and domestic legal standards. In the area of minority rights, much of current discussion centres on mechanisms rather than standards. But mechanisms need the support of coherent principles; the two are interconnected.

The coverage of minority rights in the era of the United Nations has been very thin, in sharp contrast to the range of treaties and declarations safeguarded by the League of Nations.

As James Mayall pointed out in Chapter 2, there is no reference to minorities in the UN Charter or in the Universal Declaration of Human Rights. To put it another way, the principle of universal human rights on the basis of non-discrimination on racial, ethnic, religious and other grounds was deemed to be sufficient protection for minority groups. The term 'minority' was even omitted from the lists of prohibited grounds of discrimination, though Article 14 of the European Convention on Human Rights and Fundamental Freedoms constitutes a notable exception to the general trend:

> The enjoyment of the rights and freedoms set forth in this Convention shall be secured without discrimination on any ground such as sex, race, colour, language, religion, political or other opinion,

national or social origin, association with a national minority, property, birth or other status.

Article 27

Until recently, the main burden of minority rights in general international law was borne by Article 27 of the International Covenant on Civil and Political Rights (1966):

> In those States in which ethnic, religious or linguistic minorities exist, persons belonging to such minorities shall not be denied the right, in community with the other members of their group, to enjoy their own culture, to profess and practise their own religion, or to use their own language.

This is a cautious and tentative article which reflects the very limited space that states were prepared to allow minority rights. The text prompts the following observations:

(1) Rights of minorities may not be universal rights: since the groups may not 'exist' in all states;
(2) The text refers to the rights of persons and not of groups, thus limiting the community or collective dimension of the rights;
(3) The members of minorities are not described as *having* the rights – rather, the rights 'shall not be denied' them;
(4) The article does not clearly implicate state action or resources to benefit minorities.

In *International Law and the Rights of Minorities*,[1] the present author nonetheless offered an interpretation of Article 27 which tried to overcome some of these limitations. The basis of the argument is that a purely negative reading of Article 27 does not correspond with the principle of effectiveness in the interpretation of treaties, which assumes that the article must add to other treaty principles, notably freedom of religion, equality and non-discrimination. Accordingly, the state should act to support minority cultures and not simply take the role of passive by-stander if the groups desire the continuation and flourishing of their specific characteristics and contribution to the wider society. It is also proposed that the existence of minorities is a question of fact rather than law and should not be denied by states contrary to fact. Most, if not all, states in the world have minority groups that wish to maintain their distinctiveness in the face of assimilationist pressures.

The UN Declaration of December 1992

In adopting Resolution 47/135 on 18 December 1992, the General Assembly of the United Nations completed an important phase of standard-setting in minority rights: the resolution contains the 'Declaration on the Rights of Persons Belonging to National or Ethnic, Religious and Linguistic Minorities'. The text can be regarded as a new 'international minimum standard' for minority rights, transcending some of the limitations of Article 27. The major points in the text of the Declaration are:

(1) *Article 1*: states are mandated to protect the existence and identity of minorities within their respective territories and to take appropriate measures to that effect.

(2) *Article 2.1*: the provisions of Article 27 are effectively restated and elaborated to insist that basic rights may be exercised 'in private and in public, freely and without interference or any form of discrimination'.

(3) *Articles 2.2 and 2.3*: members of minorities have wide-ranging participation rights, including the right to participate in decisions affecting them at national and regional level.

(4) *Article 2.4*: members of minorities have the right to establish and maintain their own associations, without any specific limitation as to type of association.

(5) *Article 2.5*: members of minorities have the right to maintain contacts with other group members and other minorities, as well as with kin-groups across frontiers. The safeguard for the state is that the contacts must be 'free and peaceful'.

(6) *Article 3*: rights may be exercised individually as well as in community with other members of the group, thus preventing the 'individualization' of rights by the state (e.g., through stipulations that private use of language or exercise of religion is sufficient to meet state obligations to minorities).

(7) *Article 4* deals crucially with the measures to be adopted by states to support minority rights. Despite being expressed in qualified terms, the obligations to take measures overcome much of the passivity implicit in Article 27. Among the measures are important provisions on mother-tongue instruction (Article 4.3) and injunctions to promote knowledge of minority cultures and religions existing in the state. In turn, members of minorities are encouraged to gain knowledge of the wider society, thus discouraging entirely selfish concentration on minority affairs.

(8) *Articles 5, 6 and 7* provide for minority interests to be duly accounted for in state programmes and exercises in international cooperation. The articles also touch on confidence-building and mutual understanding between states in the matter of minorities, and (in somewhat ambiguous terms) between states and groups.

(9) *Article 8* tries to link minority rights with general principles of equality, respect for the rights of other human beings, and concern for the territorial integrity of the state. It is very clear that the aim of the measures in the Declaration is not to promote secession or enhance self-determination – such questions are kept off the agenda.

(10) *Article 9* indicates that the UN system as a whole is expected to contribute to achieving the purposes of the Declaration. In practice, since the intention is to mobilize UN resources behind the Declaration, this is potentially a very important provision.

A number of general points can also be made:

(1) The title of the Declaration adds 'national' to the list of minorities in Article 27 of the Covenant, but it is not clear that this signifies any rule about whether members of minorities must have the nationality or citizenship of the states in which they 'exist'. Such a restriction, however, may flow from the minority concept itself. Germany has insisted that the Declaration is limited to nationals/ citizens, but states such as Nigeria envisage a role for the Declaration in combating hostility and prejudice against immigrants or foreigners by suggesting that it applies also to non-nationals.

(2) There is no definition of minorities at any point in the text: the Human Rights Commission Working Group which drafted the Declaration advised that the adjectives 'national, ethnic, religious and linguistic' constituted sufficient descriptions in themselves. The search for a definition stalled work on the Declaration for a number of years in the mid-1980s.

(3) Suggestions for including a right to autonomy for minorities were rejected during the drafting. Even the lower-level right of 'self-management' was not accepted. Any concept of rights for minorities prefaced by 'self-' was unacceptable to states. Concern for state sovereignty was prominent in the debates on these points.

(4) The rights apply to 'persons belonging to' minorities, not to minorities as such: they remain individual rights, though their

collective dimension is slightly more elaborate than is the case for Article 27. For example, Article 1 of the Declaration insists that states protect the existence and identity of 'minorities' and not just 'persons belonging to' minorities.

Recent European initiatives

Besides this 'global' exercise in setting human rights standards, the various European regional organizations have been attempting to develop appropriate sets of principles in a previously neglected field of law. In terms of their scope, the European instruments tend to concentrate on the single category of 'national' minorities and indicate that the nationality/citizenship element is pre-eminent in the minority concept. Some examples will suffice (see box).

The CSCE and the Council of Europe

Besides this clear limitation on the beneficiaries of the instruments, progress by the CSCE and the Council of Europe towards a regime of minority rights can be judged only a qualified success.

CSCE instruments contain important principles for minority rights and reflect the fundamental notions that minorities are a permanent feature of states as well as a source of enrichment of European society.

From a legal viewpoint, the CSCE instruments are generally progressive. But they often lack internal consistency and are not free from elements of regression. For example, the reference in the 1992 Helsinki Follow-Up Meeting to 'persons belonging to indigenous populations' is below the level of current international standards on two counts. First, indigenous rights are also collective rights and not purely individual rights; and, second, UN terminology refers to indigenous 'peoples' and not just 'populations'. The CSCE has nonetheless raised the profile of minority rights in the European framework, and its rather loose and unstructured set of standards contains a range of fundamental principles which considerably advance the minorities' case.

In many ways, the Council of Europe has not advanced greatly beyond Article 14 of the European Convention on Human Rights: the draft European Convention for the Protection of Minorities remains a draft; the European Charter for Regional or Minority Languages is structured less on the rights of minorities or their members than on state undertakings to recognize minority languages. The most promising

The meaning of 'minorities' in recent European conventions

The European Charter for Regional or Minority Languages

'Article 1 – Definitions

For the Purposes of this Charter:

a. "regional or minority languages" means languages that are

    i. traditionally used within a given territory of a State by nationals of that State who form a group numerically smaller than the rest of the State's population; and

    ii. different from the official language(s) of that State; it does not include either dialects of the official language(s) of the State or the languages of migrants.'

Proposal for a European Convention for the Protection of Minorities, prepared by the European Commission for Democracy Through Law, Strasbourg, 4 March 1991, CDL (91) 7

'Article 2.1. For the purposes of this Convention, the term "minority" shall mean a group which is smaller in number than the rest of the population of a State, whose members, who are nationals of that State, have ethnical, religious or linguistic features different from those of the rest of the population, and are guided by the will to safeguard their culture, traditions, religion or language.'

Text of the Proposal for an Additional Protocol to the Convention for the Protection of Human Rights and Fundamental Freedoms Concerning Persons Belonging to National Minorities, attached to Recommendation 1201 (1993) of the Parliamentary Assembly of the Council of Europe

'Article 1:

For the purposes of this Convention [the European Convention on Human Rights and Fundamental Freedoms], the expression "national minority" refers to a group of persons in a State who

    (a) reside on the territory of that State and are citizens thereof,

    (b) maintain long standing, firm and lasting ties with that State,

    (c) display distinctive ethnic, cultural, religious or linguistic characteristics,

    (d) are sufficiently representative, although smaller in number than the rest of the population of that State or of a region of that State,

    (e) are motivated by a concern to preserve together that which constitutes their common identity, including their culture, their traditions, their religion or their language.'

avenue of progress – the Additional Protocol to the European Convention on Human Rights – has not been finally approved by the Council of Europe machinery. The Council of Europe has recognized the extreme urgency of decisions and commitments in the field of minority rights: in Recommendation 1201 (1993) the Parliamentary Assembly of the Council looked forward to the opening for signature of a protocol on the rights of minorities at the Vienna meetings of Heads of State and Government on 8 and 9 October 1993. (For the Vienna meeting's actions, see p. 92.)

Concluding observations

The minorities question is a specific question within the general field of human rights. Minority rights are part of human rights but, like other categories and issues in human rights, they need their own particular focus.

There has been a gradual realization that the principle of non-discrimination is only a first step in the protection of minorities, but is not sufficient in itself to deal with the question.

The core of the rights of minorities in international law is their right to existence and identity. Special measures to favour the flourishing of this identity are not to be regarded as discriminatory.

International legal instruments manifest a growing respect for diversity, for the right to be different. Deliberately assimilationist policies are increasingly discouraged. A richer, more participatory concept of democracy which reflects this diversity is in the process of evolution.

The minorities issue in international law still needs to be distinguished sharply from that of self-determination. Minorities as such do not have the right to self-determination – that right is for 'peoples'. But minorities should participate in the self-determination process and not be excluded from it.

Although it is sometimes resorted to as a means of reconciling the minority and the state, the right to autonomy is not a specific right of minorities in contemporary international law. An evolution may be under way in this respect towards greater recognition of autonomy by international law. For the time being, however, we are faced with the paradoxical situation that states practising generous policies of autonomy in their internal law may be very reluctant to translate this into binding or even hortatory international norms.

There is no generally accepted definition of minorities in international law. The concept of self-definition is increasingly respected by international instruments, as is the idea that the existence of groups is a

question of fact rather than law. Both of these concepts were in fact recognized under the regime of the League of Nations and are in the process of being 'rediscovered'!

The minorities question overlaps with that of indigenous peoples. Indigenous peoples claim to be more than minorities but have been able to take advantage of rules applying to minorities. International instruments on indigenous peoples are much bolder on collective rights than are instruments on minorities. Examples are the ILO Convention 169 on Indigenous and Tribal Peoples 1989, or the draft Universal Declaration of the Rights of Indigenous Peoples contained in UN Doc. E/CN.4/Sub.2/1992/33, Annex 1. Europe is not outside the range of the definitions of indigenous peoples: the Lapps and Sami are cases in point.

Progress on the rights of minorities has been achieved more through the elaboration of a collective dimension to individual rights than through the growth of collective rights. The apparently greater readiness to allow collective rights to indigenous peoples may reflect a view that indigenous claims do not threaten states in the same way as the claims of some minorities to self-determination: in the indigenous context, self-determination is only rarely about secession.

International law is beginning to understand the minorities question better. The architecture of any eventual regime for minorities may be glimpsed as a distant building, even if the details and intricacies are not yet clear.

Notes

1 Patrick Thornberry, *International Law and the Rights of Minorities* (Oxford: Clarendon Press, 1991 and 1992).

4

NORTHERN IRELAND

TOM HADDEN

Introduction

One of the striking features of international human rights law and political practice in respect of minorities is its variability. Over the years there has been a continual and at times cyclical progression in the formulation and application of minority rights in response to changing ideologies and changing political priorities. Since this feature of law and practice in respect of minorities appears to have had some impact in Northern Ireland, it may help to begin with a brief summary of developments in international law and national practice in this sphere. An attempt will then be made to show how these developments have been mirrored in Northern Ireland. Finally some tentative conclusions will be drawn on the lessons which these developments may have for the future both of Northern Ireland and of international human rights law and practice.

Developments in human rights law and political practice

The story of human rights law can perhaps be taken to have started in the eighteenth century with an almost exclusive emphasis in the American Declaration of Independence and the French Declaration of the Rights of Man on the rights of the individual as opposed to the group or community. This may be related to the prevailing political and economic theories in which individuals were thought to be independent actors who made their own political, social and economic contracts.

During the nineteenth century there appears to have been a general shift towards the recognition of peoples and classes as primary political

and social entities to which individuals belonged, whether they liked it or not. The new science of sociology focused attention on such concepts as *volksgeist*, group psychology and class interests. This was reflected primarily in the ideals of the nation-state and class politics. But it also led to an increased interest in the identification and accommodation of minorities. The first minority protection treaties were negotiated in the Balkans towards the end of the nineteenth century.[1] The problem of how to deal with minorities which could not be fitted neatly into the newly constructed patchwork of nation-states then became one of the primary political concerns after the war of 1914–18. In some cases the preferred solution was the mass transfer of people into suitably homogeneous states, as in the case of Greeks and Turks. The more common response was the negotiation of bilateral minority treaties which had the backing of the League of Nations and were to be enforced as an integral part of international law. The distinction between individual and group rights does not appear to have been recognized as creating any major theoretical or practical difficulties during this period. But the fact that the treaties were often ignored and that the existence of ethnic minorities was used as an excuse for German aggression soon brought the concept of minority recognition into some disrepute.

After the war of 1939–45 attention shifted back again to the identification of individual human rights. The emerging consensus on international human rights law, as expressed in the Universal Declaration of Human Rights and the European Convention on Human Rights and Fundamental Freedoms, focused almost exclusively on the protection of individuals from unjustified state interference and from any form of discrimination based on group identity. The assimilation of immigrants into a tolerant liberal society was the order of the age. The only surviving reference to the rights of groups was in respect of self-determination, which probably had more to do with the pressure for decolonization than with the acceptance of the validity of group rights. It was not unusual in this period for human rights experts to deny that a human right could properly be vested in anyone but an individual. Those responsible for the formulation of Article 27 of the International Covenant on Civil and Political Rights, which was the first reassertion of the rights of minorities after a lengthy period of silence, could not bring themselves to express minority rights in other than individual terms.

More recently the pendulum has swung back again towards the recognition of group and minority rights. This has much to do with the increasing recognition of – and guilt about – the destruction of traditional

and indigenous cultures by Western societies and values. It may also be related to the re-emergence of fundamentalist religions as a powerful social and political force in many countries. It was certainly well under way before the collapse of the Soviet empire forced the issue of minority rights back into the forefront of the international political and human rights agenda. But events in former Yugoslavia and elsewhere are already causing some reaction and a reassessment of the need to protect the rights of individuals against enforced and unwanted communal separation and conflict.

The point of this brief summary of two hundred years of legal and political development is not to suggest that those involved did not recognize or understand the issues. No experienced social scientist or historian expects to find many ideas or arguments that are completely new. It is to emphasize, first, that there is a genuine difference between political and legal structures in which the principal focus is on individuals as opposed to communities or on individual as opposed to group rights, and, second, that there is a real choice to be made between them. It does not follow that there is a single correct answer to be found, any more than there is a correct position for a pendulum. But it is certainly as important for social and political scientists and for politicians and human rights lawyers to understand the nature of the cyclical processes in which they are involved as for natural scientists to understand the motion of a pendulum.

Developments in Northern Ireland

The somewhat shorter history of Northern Ireland can without too much distortion be made to reflect some of these developments in the way in which communal groups have been perceived both in international and human rights law and in political practice.

The story may likewise be taken up towards the end of the eighteenth century, by which time the patterns of settlement in Ireland were well established. In the northeastern counties the English and Scottish Protestants who had settled there in the seventeenth century were dominant both numerically and in their control over the best land and the bulk of industry and commerce. But there was continuing conflict and skirmishing between them and members of the previously established Irish community in rural areas. In the latter part of the nineteenth century this conflict and antagonism spread to Belfast as more and more Catholics moved from the west in search of employment and better living

Map 1: The basis of partition

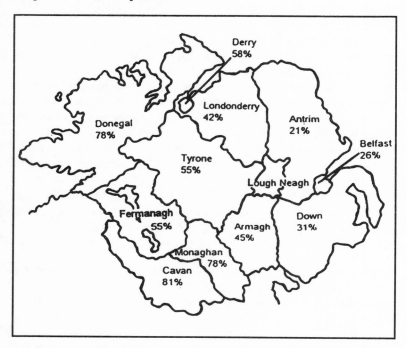

Once partition had been decided on, where should the border have been drawn? This map shows the Catholic population of the nine counties of Ulster and of Belfast and Derry as a proportion of the total population in 1901.

conditions. In the rest of Ireland the Anglo-Irish gentry and professional classes were equally dominant but were heavily outnumbered by the Catholic peasantry.

The development of the concept of a distinctive Irish people in the latter part of the nineteenth century led eventually, as in many other parts of Europe, to the creation of a new nation-state in the 1920s. But the Protestant community in the north had no real empathy with the Catholic/Irish *volksgeist* and was strong enough politically, economically and militarily to resist both home rule and inclusion in the Irish Free State. The result was partition. The new Irish state was highly homogeneous and became progressively more so, not least as a result of some ethnic purification in the 1920s. The territory assigned to Northern Ireland, however, was an ethnic frontier zone in which the two communities were inextricably intermingled.[2] In the 1920s there was a heavy predominance of Protestants in the counties of Antrim and Down, a marginal majority in most of counties Armagh and Londonderry, and rough equality in Fermanagh and Tyrone and other border areas, as shown in Map 1.

In the ensuing period both states, while purporting to comply with the limited legal protection against religious discrimination included in their constitutions, developed policies and practices designed to assimilate or minimize the influence of their respective minorities. In the Irish Free State, which later became the Irish Republic, this was relatively successful. The proportion of Protestants declined from some 10 per cent in the 1920s to fewer than 5 per cent in 1991. In Northern Ireland the fears of the Protestants over losing their majority status in the face of a consistently higher Catholic birth-rate, and the refusal of many Catholics to cooperate in the processes of government, resulted in the subordination of the ideal of assimilation to the reality of domination and exclusion. This too was effective in the sense that the natural increase in the Catholic population was offset by consistently higher emigration, due in part to discrim-ination in employment. But little progress was made in securing the consent of the Catholic community for the structures and processes of government.

The breakdown came in the late 1960s as a result of the assertion not of communal but of individual civil rights, in imitation of the civil rights movement in the United States. The leaders of the Northern Ireland Civil Rights Association were claiming their individual human rights as British citizens and not some form of separate communal recognition. But the violent reaction to these demands on the part of some Protestants

Map 2: The Catholic population in the 16 District Council areas in 1991

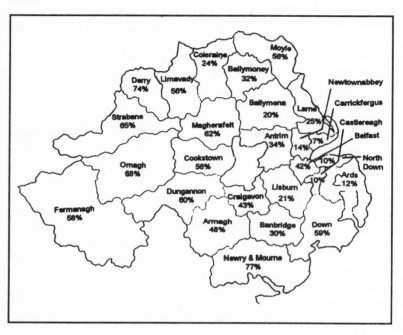

soon led to the usual unhappy combination of repression and reform and eventually to the emergence of terrorist activity in both communities. In the period from 1969 to 1992 more than three thousand people were killed and many more injured. The IRA and other nationalist paramilitaries have killed more than eight hundred members of the security forces and almost as many civilians; they have also inflicted massive damage on commercial and industrial property. Protestant paramilitaries have killed more than seven hundred Catholics, most of whom were innocent of any paramilitary involvement. More than three hundred suspected terrorists have been killed by the security forces.

The attempt to deal with this problem in the early 1970s by resorting to large-scale internment without trial was a signal failure, not least as a result of systematic abuses during arrests and subsequent interrogations by members of the security forces. But the replacement of internment by other forms of emergency law, notably provision for seven-day detention for interrogation and for trials in non-jury courts, has not led to any major decrease in complaints of human rights abuses by the security forces. There have been recurrent allegations that the Royal Ulster Constabulary (RUC), more than 90 per cent of which is recruited from the Protestant community, and the British Army have deliberately resorted to unlawful killings, torture during interrogations, the fabrication of confessions, the systematic abuse of emergency powers of arrest and search, and the general harassment of the Catholic community at large.

These 'troubles' resulted in substantial movements of population as members of both communities withdrew from mixed areas, driven by a mixture of fear and of direct intimidation. Though the largest movement was in the early 1970s in Belfast,[3] the process has continued more gradually since then. But the result has been the creation of many more communally 'pure' estates and suburbs rather than any major change in the overall intermingling of the two communities. The latest figures on the distribution of population in 1991, as shown in Map 2, show little change in the overall pattern of overwhelming Protestant predominance in the east, declining gradually to equality and Catholic predominance in border areas, despite a noticeable increase in the overall proportion of Catholics to a current figure of some 45 per cent.

The search for a political settlement

At a political level the initial response of the British government to the renewed outbreak of communal conflict in 1968 was to put pressure on

the incumbent and exclusively Unionist administration to eliminate all forms of discrimination against Catholics. When the deteriorating security situation led to the imposition of 'direct rule' from London in 1972, this policy was extended to include the creation of a devolved government which would contain elected representatives from both communities. With the cooperation of the Irish government this was achieved for a short period in 1974. But the new 'power-sharing' administration was brought down within months by a political strike within the Protestant community which the authorities failed to contain. After another unsuccessful attempt in 1975 to get the local political parties to agree on new structures for devolved self-government, the British government abandoned its efforts and fell back on a strategy of what is intended to be benevolent and impartial rule from London.

In the 1980s both the British and the Irish governments committed themselves more openly and explicitly to a policy of recognizing and accommodating the existence of two separate communities. The process culminated in the Anglo-Irish Agreement of 1985, which may be described for the purposes of this study as a bilateral minority or communal rights treaty. But this has not led as yet to any observable increase in the willingness of the elected representatives of the two communities to agree to a grand compromise on some form of local democratic government, as had been hoped; rather, it has given rise to increased demands for various forms of special recognition and accommodation on a communal basis. The political objectives of the major Catholic party, the Social Democratic and Labour Party (SDLP), have apparently escalated from demands for power-sharing at a regional level to some form of joint British–Irish authority over Northern Ireland. There are also increasing demands for greater cultural recognition and provision, not least for Irish-language activities, and for the creation of separate communal police forces. The 'talks process' initiated in 1990 with a view to replacing the 1985 Agreement with a more generally acceptable settlement has yet to produce any consensus which might lead to the peace and stability that was the primary objective of the bilateral Anglo-Irish initiative.

The impact of human rights
Most aspects of this continuing conflict and many of the demands of the minority Catholic community can be related to one or more of the provisions of existing or draft international human rights declarations or covenants on individual or minority rights. But international human

rights law has rarely provided an unequivocal answer. On many issues the British government and the representatives of the majority Protestant community have been able to claim equivalent or countervailing rights.

The right to self-determination

It will not come as any surprise to students of divided societies that the supposedly fundamental right of self-determination has contributed to, rather than assisted in resolving, the conflict. One of the primary motive forces for the continuing armed struggle by the Provisional IRA has been the alleged right of the Irish people as a whole to exercise self-determination to rid themselves of all vestiges of British rule in the island of Ireland. This claim is reflected and arguably given some support by the initial articles of the Irish constitution of 1937, which assert a formal though equivocal claim to the territory of Northern Ireland. The problem is that the Protestant community in Northern Ireland also asserts its right to self-determination, relying on the formal guarantee in successive British Acts of Parliament that the status of Northern Ireland can be decided only by the people of Northern Ireland.[4]

There is no simple resolution in human rights law to these conflicting claims. It can reasonably be argued that both the nationalist community in Ireland as a whole and the unionist community in Northern Ireland meet the accepted criteria to qualify as a people for the purposes of self-determination, namely:

(a) a distinctive language, culture or religion;
(b) a shared sense of history;
(c) a commitment to maintain their communal identity;
(d) an association with a defined territory.[5]

But in cases where two peoples or communities with different aspirations are inextricably intermingled, as in Northern Ireland, the usual forms of self-determination, whether by establishing a separate state or by merging with another, cannot be wholly satisfactory, since the aspirations of one or other must inevitably be denied. The alternative of partition is no more satisfactory unless substantial movements of population can be achieved on a voluntary basis. In such cases the concept of self-determination must be applied in a very different way if it is not to exacerbate rather than assist in resolving conflict. Some of the possibilities will be discussed further below.

Protection from the abuse of emergency laws

Complaints of the systematic abuse of the basic human rights of members of the nationalist community have played a major role in sustaining the communal conflict in Northern Ireland. A major area for concern has always been the allegedly abusive operation of emergency laws introduced to deal with communal disturbances and later with paramilitary and terrorist activity. In the initial period of communal disturbances the complaints were of bias against civil rights protesters and Catholics by the largely Protestant RUC and the exclusively Protestant auxiliaries known as the B Specials. After the deployment of the British Army in 1969 and the disbandment of the B Specials in 1970, complaints centred on general harassment by soldiers in nationalist areas. The mass internment operation of August 1971, undertaken in an attempt to stem the rise of terrorist activity and directed almost exclusively against Catholics, gave rise to widespread complaints of assaults during arrest and torture during interrogations. Since then there have been continuing complaints on a wide range of issues, including the unlawful use of lethal force, an alleged 'shoot to kill' policy by undercover army and police special units, the use of potentially lethal rubber and plastic bullets in controlling riots and confrontations, systematic arrests under emergency legislation for intelligence-gathering purposes, ill-treatment during prolonged interrogation under emergency legislation, the suspension of jury trial for terrorist offences, undue reliance on confessions obtained during interrogation as the sole basis for convictions, and the refusal to grant special status or formal segregation to politically motivated offenders in prison.[6]

It has not been easy within the British legal tradition to find effective ways of resolving these matters. The absence of any entrenched rights within the unwritten British constitution and the fact that many of the practices have been directly or indirectly authorized by emergency legislation have made it difficult for the courts to intervene, even if they had wished to do so. In practice the judges, particularly in the House of Lords in London, have been reluctant to find ways of intervening on the general ground that decisions on matters of national security must be left to the executive.

Parliament has been equally ineffective. The general approach of most MPs has been to give the benefit of any doubt to the security forces in dealing with what is by any standards a sustained and threatening terrorist campaign. When public concern on particular issues demanded some response, the government typically initiated an official inquiry with terms of reference limited to alterations in law or practice rather

than aimed at giving an effective remedy for past abuses, though in many cases claims for compensation to victims have been settled on an informal basis.[7] More recently the tendency has been to appoint commissioners, often on a non-statutory basis, to make regular reports on matters of concern.[8] The suspicion remains that the authorities are reluctant to permit fully independent scrutiny or adjudication of alleged abuses, particularly where undercover operations are in any way involved.

Dissatisfaction with the response to allegations of human rights abuses at national level has led to an increasing number of cases being referred for international adjudication under the European Convention on Human Rights. But here too the response has been equivocal. Decisions against the United Kingdom have been made in respect of the ill-treatment of suspects under interrogation in 1971 and the operation of seven-day detention for interrogation without a formal derogation in 1989.[9] But in many other cases complaints have been rejected and the authorities have been at least partially vindicated. The use of internment without trial in 1971, the use of plastic bullets for riot control in 1976, the refusal of concessions to IRA prisoners demanding special status in 1980, the use of lethal force against suspected terrorists attempting to drive through a roadblock in 1985, and the entry of a derogation to legitimize continuing seven-day detention following a previous Court decision against it have all been approved by the Commission or the Court.[10] In all these cases both the Commission and the Court have been willing to grant the government a wide margin of appreciation in adopting special measures to deal with terrorism and associated disorders.

The lesson from experience in Northern Ireland in matters of this kind is that the application of minimum acceptable international standards in human rights is unlikely to be sufficient to meet the legitimate expectations of many uncommitted members of the communities in conflict. If communal feelings of alienation from the state's law enforcement system are to be reduced, ways must be found to give international support for and appropriate monitoring of somewhat more demanding standards.

Discrimination
Complaints of discrimination against members of the Catholic community in respect of housing, employment and political representation in certain areas figured prominently in the initial civil rights campaign in the 1960s. Since then legislative and administrative action has been taken on all these matters. Most major problems have been eliminated in respect of housing by the establishment of a non-political regional public

housing agency. But despite the introduction of some of the strongest anti-discrimination laws and enforcement structures in Europe, the level of differentiation between the two communities in respect of employment has remained remarkably stable. Though a good deal of progress has been made in some areas of public and private sector employment by regular monitoring of recruitment, the unemployment rate for Catholic males in the 1990s is still, as it was in the 1970s and 1980s, more than twice that for Protestant males. Much of the problem stems from the gross imbalance in employment in the security forces and related occupations, which is due partly to general reluctance among Catholics to join the forces of what they perceive as an alien state and partly to fear of being singled out for assassination by the IRA and the consequent need for those who do accept such employment to minimize their contacts with family and friends in their own community. The problems of discrimination in employment and the perception of the police and other security forces as biased against the Catholic community are thus closely intertwined and all the more intractable. The final major area of discrimination in the political sphere has been resolved on an individual basis by the removal of some relatively minor inequalities in the voting system and some more significant manipulation of electoral boundaries. But this has not made much impact on the the larger and more important question of how to achieve and to guarantee effective participation by representatives of both communities in the structures of government.

Communal rights

As in some other divided societies, the increasing focus on measuring the extent of individual discrimination has been associated with growing pressures for the positive recognition of group or communal rights. In Northern Ireland the main focus of attention has been on cultural and educational provision, notably on the use of the Irish language and some long-standing inequalities in public spending on the essentially Protestant state school system and the separate and somewhat more independent Catholic school system.[11] There have also been demands for more formal recognition of the existence and separate identity of the two major communities. The Anglo-Irish Agreement has made some initial moves in this direction by including in its Preamble a paragraph 'recognising and respecting the identities of the two communities in Northern Ireland and the right of each to pursue its aspirations by peaceful and constitutional means', and providing in Article 5 for the Anglo-Irish Intergovernmental Conference to 'concern itself with measures to recognise and

accommodate the rights and identities of the two traditions in Northern Ireland'. Thus far this has not led to the introduction of any formal constitutional or legislative provisions for separate communal rights or representation. But there is continuing interest in ideas for express constitutional protections for certain basic communal rights.

Communal separation or communal intermingling?

This brief account of developments to date raises the question of whether the swing of the human rights pendulum towards ever greater recognition of communal as opposed to individual rights is likely to assist or impede the achievement of a peaceful resolution to more than twenty-five years of internal conflict in Northern Ireland since 1968.

Development of the idea of communal rights clearly has the potential to encourage further communal separation and may lead eventually to demands for some form of repartition to achieve the kind of communal purification which has been the objective in other ethnic conflicts. The major difficulty with this approach in Northern Ireland is that the two communities cannot easily be separated into distinct areas, despite the major population movements since the early 1970s. Though areas like West Belfast, Derry City and South Armagh are now almost exclusively Catholic and nationalist, the bulk of the territory is still shared. Those who think in terms of a new partition along the course of the Blackwater and Bann rivers, for example, on the grounds that there is now a majority of Catholics west of that line, must remember that more than one-third of the population in that area is still Protestant. There is also a significant numerical concentration of Catholics in what might be called Greater West Belfast, which could not easily be excluded from the area of a smaller and more communally pure Northern Ireland. Thoroughgoing communal purification would still require massive movements of population, whether voluntary, officially induced or forced. The only alternative means of giving effective self-determination or self-government to the two communities would appear to be some form of non-spatial allocation of powers over such matters as education, planning, local services, employment promotion and some aspects of policing.

Those who are frightened at the prospect of this kind of development are now beginning to stage a counter-attack based on the proposition that the extent and desirability of communal separation can be overstated and that the rights and interests of the large section of the population which wishes to continue to live together in peace should not be subordinated to the

Table 4.1: Communal differences in Northern Ireland

	Protestants	Catholics	Others
Percentage of total:			
Population (1991)	48.2	41.4	10.4*
Unemployed (1991)			
Male	9	23	NR
Female	6	11	NR
Household income			
(weekly average)			
(1985–7 FES)	£228.00	£185.00	NR
(1992 FES)	£290.00	£265.00	£308.00
School enrolment (1992)			
Primary	94,414**	96,047**	2,070†
Secondary	40,945**	45,282**	1,850†
Grammar	33,192**	23,678**	

* The figures for 'others' include both those who stated they had no religion and those who refused to state their religion.

**These figures are for school management types; rather more Catholics attend Protestant schools than vice versa.

†The figures are for integrated schools in 1993.

Sources: 1991 Census; 1991 Labour Force Survey; Policy Planning Research Unit (PPRU) Monitor 3/92 and 2/93; Family Expenditure Survey; School Performance Information 1991/92.

more extreme claims of the communal purists. This has led to an interesting debate on the extent to which Northern Ireland can accurately be analysed in terms of what is known as the 'internal communal conflict' theory.

There can be no doubt that Northern Ireland can be described as a highly divided society in social, economic and political terms. A recent summary of the statistical evidence showed that in terms of political solidarity the two main sections of the community in Northern Ireland were more clearly defined and separated than in any other comparable divided society.[12] Everyone in Northern Ireland is certainly accustomed to thinking about and analysing every aspect of the situation in terms of the numbers or proportions of Protestants or Catholics. There is continuing debate on the precise balance between the numbers of Protestants and Catholics and likely future trends. There is continuing concern over differentials in employment and unemployment and related differentials in household income and general prosperity. The educational system remains highly segregated. And most opinion polls are analysed in terms of the response by Protestants and Catholics to the issues in question. Some salient statistics on these matters are set out in Table 4.1.

This separation between the two communities is also reflected in current voting patterns. About 85 per cent of those who vote regularly choose parties which are clearly identified as Catholic/nationalist or Protestant/unionist, and only about 15 per cent choose parties which promote themselves as cross-communal. For example, in the 1992 Westminster election, on the first-past-the-post system, the main unionist parties secured 51 per cent of the total vote (Official Unionists 35 per cent, Democratic Unionists 13 per cent, Popular Unionists 3 per cent); the main nationalist parties 34 per cent (SDLP 24 per cent, Sinn Fein 10 per cent); and cross-communal parties 15 per cent (Alliance 9 per cent, Conservatives 6 per cent). In the most recent local elections in 1989, on the single transferable vote system, unionist parties polled 54 per cent of first preferences, nationalist parties 33 per cent and others 13 per cent.

The major criticism of this type of thinking and analysis is that it can exaggerate and perhaps accentuate the degree of division and separation. Compilation of the relevant statistics typically involves the classification of as many individuals or households as possible as either Protestant or Catholic. It therefore tends to conceal or minimize the substantial number of individuals or households which cannot sensibly or do not wish to be allocated to either. These include mixed marriages and others with close relatives in both communities, those who come from Britain and further afield and those who reject or wish to escape from any such attribution. Though there is little hard statistical evidence on these matters, there can be no doubt that there is and has always been much more intermingling of the two communities than the communal separation theory would suggest. It seems likely that up to about one-third of the population may fall into mixed, integrated or non-communal categories of this kind. This is reflected in numerous surveys which have indicated that at least one-third of the population favours integration in education and in housing, and by implication a greater degree of integration in other matters. Though these estimates may appear to be at variance with the political voting patterns outlined above, they are not necessarily so. Large numbers of people who reject communal labels may abstain from voting on the grounds that there is little point in doing so. And large numbers of those who vote for largely communal parties may nonetheless prefer integration rather than separation.

It would not be sensible to attempt to draw any firm conclusion on the extent to which any analysis in terms of communal separation must be revised to take account of this perspective. The degree of separation and intermingling and its acceptance or recognition is highly variable and in

an important sense is a matter of choice. In times of stress and open conflict those who favour communal separation or purification are likely to prevail over those who favour intermingling or integration. As has already been indicated, this was most clearly observable in Northern Ireland in the early 1970s, when there were massive movements of population in Belfast and other towns. At the present time the pressures towards separation and intermingling or integration are more evenly balanced and may be influenced either way by internal political developments, by the policies of the British and Irish governments, and ultimately by current trends in international human rights law and practice.

Future prospects

The nature of the choice facing those involved in deciding or influencing future developments in Northern Ireland may best be explained by sketching briefly two alternative objectives – the acceptance of increasing communal separation on the one hand, and the maintenance and development of pluralist structures in which members of both communities may participate on the other – and by discussing some of the ways in which they might be brought about.

Under a *communal separation* model it would be expected that members of the two communities would continue the trend towards separation in physical and institutional terms that has been observed since 1968. This would almost certainly involve further residential segregation, with Protestants withdrawing from the western counties to their communal heartland in the east, and Catholics in that area withdrawing into well-defined enclaves such as West Belfast and equivalent areas in other larger towns. It would probably involve the further development of separate agencies for the administration of public services, on the model of the recently established Catholic Maintained Schools Council. It would also be likely to require substantial changes to anti-discrimination legislation so that effective segregation in employment would become wholly acceptable. It might eventually lead to the reorganization of local government and policing on a cantonal basis so that each community would have control over its own affairs. Ultimately it could lead to a repartition settlement under which new boundaries would be established for an almost exclusively Protestant Northern Ireland and the rest of its existing territory would be absorbed into the Irish Republic. On this approach the concept of self-determination would in effect be applied separately to each community.

This scenario might be brought about in a number of different ways. The most abrupt would probably be a unilateral British decision to withdraw from Northern Ireland, whether in the context of an agreement with the Republic on reunification or as the result of a decision to transfer sovereignty to an independent Northern Ireland. In either case the probable outcome would be that the established locally recruited Protestant police and paramilitary forces would compete with the IRA and other Catholic forces for control over territory. There would certainly be a large number of refugees on either side, and if there was international intervention the situation might develop in a similar way to what has occurred in Bosnia. A similar result might also be brought about more gradually and peacefully by deliberate governmental decisions to accept and even to facilitate the process of social, economic and political separation.

The alternative scenario is one in which Northern Ireland would *continue as a unit of government* within which every attempt would be made to encourage cooperation between the two communities and to maintain institutions in which representatives of both could share power. This would be likely to involve the continuation of measures to ensure that employment in all major public and private sectors was equitably shared between Protestants and Catholics and to encourage the integration of members of both communities (and of neither) in other ways, notably in education, residential housing and leisure activities. But the objective would be to achieve mutual recognition and accommodation of the respective political and cultural traditions of both major communities rather than any form of assimilation. On this approach the right to self-determination of several peoples intermingled in a non-homogeneous territory would be interpreted as giving a right to members of both communities, and those who adhere to neither, to participate in shared structures rather than a right to separate communal autonomy.

This approach was built into the Anglo-Irish Agreement of 1985. It has been reaffirmed in the Joint Downing Street Declaration by the British and Irish governments in December 1993. In an attempt to persuade the Provisional IRA to abandon its campaign of violence, this Declaration laid particular emphasis on the issue of self-determination and on the absence of any continuing strategic or economic British interest in retaining Northern Ireland as part of the United Kingdom. However, the fact that both governments felt bound to maintain the position that the right of self-determination for the people of Ireland was subject to the concurrent right of the people of Northern Ireland to accept or reject the unification of Ireland has made it difficult for Sinn Fein or

the IRA to accept the Declaration, since they are committed to the view that the people of Northern Ireland have no separate right of self-determination. It seems unlikely, therefore, that the 'peace first' strategy of seeking to achieve a cessation of violence by paramilitaries on both sides in advance of any agreement on the nature of a longer-term political settlement will prove successful. It also seems unlikely that the indefinite prolongation of the talks process between the two governments and those parties which reject the use of violence will on its own be sufficient to achieve a settlement, since the leaders of the main parties have shown themselves to be remarkably reluctant to agree any such grand compromise. It is possible that some internal democratic pressure might be put on them to do so by means of a formal referendum on a package of measures designed to attract support both from the less extreme wings of both communities and from the non-aligned, or alternatively by imposing some economic pressures on the population as a whole. But if the parties and their committed supporters continue to resist all such pressures it may be necessary for the two governments to agree such a package between themselves and to develop a stronger form of joint authority over Northern Ireland than is provided under the consultation procedures agreed in 1985.

If this general approach is accepted, there are two significant implications. The first is that Irish unification in the immediate future is not a realistic objective. Given that a substantial minority of Catholics vote for parties which support continued unity with the United Kingdom and that almost no Protestants vote for nationalist parties, a majority vote within the whole of Northern Ireland for a change in status by a border poll remains a distant prospect. And any attempt to impose unification, even if a marginal majority were to vote for it, would be likely to increase the tendency towards communal separation and a resulting concentration of the Protestant community in the Greater Belfast area. This would in turn increase their capacity to resist such a change in status and to argue for a new partition, even if it would not justify a claim to a separate communal right to self-determination.

The second implication is that while the two communities remain intermingled, Northern Ireland is likely to require treatment as a distinct unit of government, whether within the United Kingdom or within an expanded Irish Republic. The claims of the Catholic community within Northern Ireland to be entitled to special protections and special provisions in a UK context to ensure effective participation in government would be mirrored by equivalent claims from the Protestant community

in an all-Ireland state. This would be likely to require at the least a form of federation with substantial devolution of power to a Northern Ireland region, continued provision for the maintenance of British citizenship for those who wished it, and perhaps a continuing role for the British government similar to that granted to the Irish government under the Anglo-Irish Agreement. The problems of managing a region in which two major communities with different self-perceptions and different aspirations were intermingled would certainly not disappear merely by a transfer of formal sovereignty from the United Kingdom to the Irish Republic.

The role of external actors
The primary actors in making choices between these various forms of sharing and separation are the people of Northern Ireland. They can vote, while the current constitutional arrangements persist, to remain in the United Kingdom or to join the Irish Republic. They can support or reject local parties which are prepared to share political power. Their views could be sought in one or more indicative referendums on various realistic packages. But the idea that people in either community have effective power to determine such matters is problematic. Where popular opinion is deeply divided, a simple majority vote is an unsatisfactory means of resolving conflict. In such circumstances the real power to make or prevent the making of compromise deals often rests with political representatives and paramilitaries who do not always want or need to reflect majority opinion. And on many issues people in Northern Ireland, whether as voters, politicians or paramilitaries, have very little effective power. The British and Irish governments and peoples also have important and potentially determinant roles to play in future developments. The international community in Europe and further afield may likewise have an important influence on the framework within which a resolution is sought.

The *British and Irish governments*, which must in a similar way be taken as acting in the context of current political, media and popular opinion, face the same broad choice of strategies. As in other conflicts arising out of the intermingling of two peoples in an ethnic frontier zone, they can allow themselves to be drawn by the more passionate representatives of their frontier people into adopting uncompromising attitudes and policies; or they can use their power and influence to encourage compromise.[13]

The British government has moved somewhat further in this direction than the Irish government. The Downing Street Declaration has made it abundantly clear to all that the British government has ceased to support and represent the demands of unionists in Northern Ireland in the way it did in the period leading up to partition in 1921. There is little doubt that this is an accurate reflection of public opinion throughout Great Britain. But it is less clear that the Irish government and people have ceased to give at least some tacit support to those nationalists in Northern Ireland who are committed to absolutist views of Irish unification, as shown by the reluctance to abandon the irredentist provisions of Articles 2 and 3 of the Irish constitution in advance of a settlement which reflects those claims in some other way. There is a similar difficulty, which is built into the Anglo-Irish Agreement, over the continuing tendency on the part of the Irish government to represent only the interests of the nationalist community in Northern Ireland, as opposed to those of the population as a whole. This imbalance in the approach of the British and Irish governments to the future of Northern Ireland is currently one of the major impediments to agreement on shared structures for government within Northern Ireland. So, too, is the continuing reluctance of the British government to abandon those aspects of an absolutist notion of sovereignty which place a barrier on its acceptance of more independent judicial control and external monitoring of some aspects of its security operations in Northern Ireland.

The role of the international community in general and of European bodies such as the European Union, the Council of Europe and the CSCE is necessarily more limited. If the British and Irish governments cannot devise and deliver a peaceful settlement in Northern Ireland, it is unlikely that the international community could intervene to any better effect. The promise of a United Nations peacekeeping force to replace British troops in Northern Ireland in the absence of an agreed settlement would be likely, as in most other equivalent UN operations, to signal the beginning of a period of communal separation and territorial consolidation by the main paramilitary forces, rather than a more serious search for compromise. A better approach for interested states and international bodies may be to offer their good offices in guaranteeing and monitoring a settlement achieved by the United Kingdom and the Irish Republic.

The role of the *European Union* in this context is likely to be restricted to the recognition of Northern Ireland as a special border region and the provision of appropriate financial and economic support. The EU has to date been reluctant to play any major political role in negotiating

constitutional changes in areas of dispute between its member states. It has shown little interest in the proposal by the SDLP that the EU should nominate a commissioner to share the government of Northern Ireland with nominees of the British and Irish governments and three locally elected representatives. Nor is there much prospect, while the EU remains an association of states, of the recognition of Northern Ireland, or any other similarly disputed frontier zone, as a region with special status outside the territory of any one member state. And though it would be formally possible for the EU to guarantee a new British–Irish Agreement by becoming a party to it or by accepting it as a protocol to the Treaty of Rome or the Maastricht Treaty of European Union, this also might be seen as too dangerous a precedent to be generally acceptable.

The primary role of the *Council of Europe* is likely to be in helping to guarantee and adjudicate on the individual and communal rights aspects of any new settlement. It appears to be generally accepted that formal adjudication on human rights issues should be left to the Commission and Court of Human Rights at Strasbourg rather than taken over by the EU or any newly constituted body. For example, the creation of a special court with representatives from the Commission and Court in Strasbourg to adjudicate on individual and communal rights in Bosnia has been informally approved by the relevant Council of Europe institutions as part of the Vance–Owen plan for Bosnia. Though the future of this proposal remains uncertain at the time of writing, the precedent could be built on in the context of a new British–Irish Agreement over Northern Ireland. Some form of recognition by the Council of Europe of the terms of the human rights elements in a new agreement, and the possibility of referring disputes to an independent external adjudicatory body distinct from the British and Irish courts, might assist in giving confidence to both sides in Northern Ireland on the validity of any individual and communal rights provisions in a new British–Irish Agreement.

The human rights provisions within the *CSCE* are in some respects, notably on the protection of minorities, more developed and specific than those of the Council of Europe. The Copenhagen Document of 1990 sets out a number of significant principles of particular relevance to Northern Ireland: that 'persons belonging to national minorities have the right freely to express, preserve and develop their ethnic, cultural, linguistic or religious identity and to maintain and develop their culture in all its aspects, free of any attempts at assimilation against their will'; that there may be a need for 'special measures' to ensure full equality for members of minorities; and that minority communities have the right to establish

educational and cultural institutions within the state and contacts with common communities across national frontiers, and to effective participation in national affairs.

Though the CSCE process does not provide for any formal adjudication on these matters, it does provide under the so-called Vienna and Moscow mechanisms[14] for diplomatic intervention by participating states and for the appointment of missions of experts to visit and report on the situation in territories in which there are human rights concerns. Provision has also been made in the Helsinki Final Act of 1992 for the appointment of a High Commissioner for Minorities to monitor the performance of participating states on the treatment of minorities. These new monitoring structures could be used to provide additional international safeguards against any continuing human rights abuses by security forces and to ensure that the Copenhagen principles on minority rights were being effectively adhered to in any new settlement in Northern Ireland. The British government, however, has entered a reservation to the Moscow mechanism, to the effect that on security grounds it might refuse to allow a mission of experts to visit particular areas, and the terms of reference for the High Commissioner for Minorities specifically exclude any intervention in situations involving terrorism.[15] It would clearly be desirable as a means of generating confidence in a new settlement for Northern Ireland if there could be agreement that international monitoring under the CSCE process would be accepted without reservation in respect of both minority protection and human rights generally.

Lessons from Northern Ireland
Only a few tentative conclusions can be drawn on the implications of developments in Northern Ireland for international human rights law and political practice in respect of minorities.

One is that it may not always be helpful to talk in terms of majority and minority rights. It has often been pointed out that Northern Ireland is a classic case of a 'double minority' in that the dominant or subordinate status of either community depends on where the boundaries are drawn. It may also become an example of a situation in which two (or more) communities are evenly balanced and in which provision for simple majority decision-making on many issues may be inappropriate. The underlying issue for human rights lawyers is what rights both individuals and communities are entitled to assert in the face of whatever form of 'democratic' decision-making is provided for within a particular state.

Dealing with this issue may not be made easier by the introduction of the concepts of majorities and minorities.

A second conclusion is that the approach in most international covenants and declarations on minority (or communal) rights is often unclear and unhelpful in many respects. There is clearly a need for clarification of the application of the right to self-determination in situations in which two or more communities are intermingled. There is also a need for more detailed provisions on the issues of communal recognition and permissible forms of positive discrimination. Progress on all these issues may well require the development of more practical and pragmatic guidelines on appropriate or permissible measures in particular situations. In this context it is likely to be necessary to distinguish more clearly between communities (or minorities) of different sizes, types and distributions in relation to the population at large.

A final and more general conclusion is that it may be helpful for international human rights declarations and covenants to deal more openly with the flexibility of human rights standards in this area. This is likely to involve greater recognition of the essentially political choices which are involved in dealing with the balance between individual and communal rights, rather than continuing to imply that both are in some sense absolute. As has already been suggested, on matters of this kind the human rights pendulum swings to and fro over time. Just as economists have to come to terms with the need to understand and manage the business cycle as best they can, so must human rights lawyers come to terms with the need to understand and manage the swings of the pendulum between individual and communal rights.

Notes

Much of this paper is based on a project which I have undertaken in collaboration with Professor Kevin Boyle of the University of Essex. A full account is published under our joint names in *Northern Ireland – The Choice* (Harmondsworth: Penguin Books, 1994); I should like to acknowledge his contribution to and comments on this particular presentation of our ideas.

1 Henri Giordan (ed.), *Les Minorités en Europe* (Paris: Kimé, 1992).
2 Frank Wright, *Northern Ireland: A Comparative Analysis* (Dublin: Gill and Macmillan, 1988).
3 Northern Ireland Community Relations Commission Research Unit, *Flight: A Recent Report on Publication Movement in Belfast during August 1971* (Belfast: Northern Ireland Community Relations Commission, 1972).

4   Irish Free State (Agreement) Act, 1922, s.1; Ireland Act, 1949, s.1; Northern Ireland Constitution Act, 1973, s.l.

5   See *Report of the Special Rapporteur on the Historical and Current Development of the Right to Self-Determination* (Critescu Report), UN Doc E/CN.4/Sub.2/404/Rev.1, 1981.

6   For a useful summary of issues in this area see Anthony Jennings (ed.), *Justice Under Fire* (London: Pluto Press, 2nd edn, 1989).

7   See for example the report of the Widgery Tribunal into the 'Bloody Sunday' shootings in Londonderry on 30 January 1972 (1971–72 H.C.220) and the report of the Bennett Committee into RUC interrogation procedures (1979 Cmnd. 7497).

8   Commissioners have been appointed to review the operation of emergency powers, to supervise interrogation centres, and to monitor complaints against the Army.

9   *Ireland v UK* (1982), 4 European Human Rights Report 40; *Brogan v UK* (1989), 11 EHRR 117.

10 *Ireland v UK* (above); *McFeely v UK* (1981), 3 EHRR 161; *Stewart v UK* (1985), 7 EHRR 453; *Kelly v UK*, 13 January 1993; *Brannigan & McBride v UK*, 26 May 1993.

11 See the 17th Report of the Standing Advisory Commission on Human Rights, ch. 2.

12 John Whyte, *Interpreting Northern Ireland* (Oxford: Clarendon Press, 1991), p. 73.

13 This important insight was developed in Wright, op. cit.

14 The Vienna mechanism (agreed in January 1989) enables CSCE member states to monitor observance and human dimension commitments by a procedure involving (a) exchange of information, (b) bilateral meetings, (c) drawing the attention of other member states to 'cases' or 'situations', and (d) bringing the matter to a full CSCE conference.

   The Moscow mechanism (agreed in 1991) provides for the CSCE to send experts to monitor adherence to human dimension commitments. In circumstances where the challenged state is uncooperative, the CSCE can still send a mission (on the 'consensus minus one' principle).

15 It was stated at the Chatham House workshop that the reservation to the Moscow mechanism was not intended to exclude CSCE missions from Northern Ireland and that the restriction on the powers of the High Commissioner had been insisted on by the Turkish and Spanish governments rather than the British government.

5

SOUTH TYROL

ANTONY ALCOCK

Introduction

The South Tyrol autonomy has been hailed as one of the best examples of the protection of regional and cultural minorities in the world. Indeed the experiences of the German-speaking South Tyrolese in finally achieving that autonomy after many years has led them on from continuous battles with the Italian authorities to advocating far-reaching guidelines for autonomies for the minorities in central and eastern Europe, including the countries of the former Soviet Union.[1]

Nevertheless it has to be pointed out that success took 46 years to achieve. The so-called De Gasperi–Gruber Agreement, named after the Foreign Ministers of Italy and Austria respectively, was made in 1946; but it was not until the summer of 1992 that the Austrian government issued a statement that the Italian government had finally implemented the package of reforms agreed between the two governments and the Südtiroler Volkspartei, or SVP, in December 1969. This statement was made on the advice of the South Tyrolese (as expressed by the SVP, which regularly obtains 90 per cent of the German-speaking vote).

The South Tyrol question had a relatively successful outcome largely because the main objectives of both the Italian state and the South Tyrolese minority were, on the whole, achieved. The chief concern of the Italian government in Rome, the Italian-dominated regional government of Trentino–Alto Adige (one of the five Italian regions with a special statute) and the Italian community in the province of South Tyrol was the maintenance of the security and integrity of the Italian state. The principal concern of the South Tyrolese minority was its own cultural, economic and social development, seen in terms of being able to flourish in its own homeland.

The struggle for autonomy

But why should the relatively satisfactory resolution of the South Tyrol question have taken so long? The answer is that the question of the security and integrity of the Italian state was not immediately settled in 1946. For one thing, the De Gasperi–Gruber Agreement did not contain a renunciation of South Tyrol by Austria. Moreover, statements by Austrian (and particularly North Tyrolese) politicians to the effect that the situation was only temporary, as well as South Tyrolese open anger at the failure to achieve self-determination,[2] led the Italian government not only to provide a very restricted autonomy[3] for South Tyrol but to apply it restrictively.

First, obliged to consult the South Tyrolese about the form of the autonomy under the terms of the Agreement, Rome did so only minimally and perfunctorily. Austria, under Four-Power occupation, was helpless. The South Tyrolese were asked to comment on Italian draft statutes and even submitted one of their own, but their views were ignored. There were a couple of short meetings, but no dialogue, let alone any consensus.

Second, to overcome Italian fears that the South Tyrolese, who comprised two-thirds of the population of South Tyrol, would predominate in the Provincial Assembly, the province of South Tyrol was combined with the 99 per cent Italian province of Trento to form the region Trentino–Alto Adige; the population of the whole region was two-thirds Italian.

Third, it was the region that was given primary legislative powers regarding the main sectors of the economy – agriculture and tourism – and secondary legislative powers in regard to industrial development. The South Tyrolese were given primary powers relating to such matters as place names, fairs and markets, inland harbours, first aid and accident services. They were also given legislative powers with regard to housing, but since the province had no money to build houses this very important power was – as will be seen – valueless.

Finally, through decisions of, first, the Council of State and then, after its establishment, the Constitutional Court, the provincial autonomy of South Tyrol was restrictively interpreted and applied. For example, the region's administrative powers were not automatically devolved to the provinces as had been expected and 'normally' provided for in the 1948 Regional Autonomy Statute, and the failure to do this was upheld by the Constitutional Court.[4] The South Tyrolese had expected ethnic proportionality to prevail in public employment (the 1946 Agreement had

spoken of 'reaching a more appropriate proportion of employment between the two ethnical groups'), but under various Italian rulings this was to apply only to regional and provincial offices, and not to state bodies operating in South Tyrol, such as the state railways and post and telegraph services, while semi-state bodies such as health insurance companies were required to reflect in their staffs merely the ethnic proportions of their clients and not the size of the German group as a whole.[5]

All this adversely affected the economic and social development of the South Tyrolese. Very much a mountain farming people, they were now hit by the 'flight from the land' that was such a common feature of Europe in the 1950s. But there were no jobs to be obtained in the administration for the reasons given above. They had little experience and no incentive to go into the Italian-dominated industrial sector deliberately set up by the Fascists in the 1930s to alter the economic and demographic structure of South Tyrol. Jobs in commerce implied moving to the towns, but that required housing, and the allocation of public housing built with Italian state funds took account of the ethnic proportions of the municipal population in question. Since the two leading towns in South Tyrol had Italian majorities (Bolzano 80 per cent, Merano 60 per cent), housing quotas were filled on that basis. Indeed, the expansion of Italian industry and a commensurate housing policy were Rome's chief weapons in the defence of the *italianità* of South Tyrol.

The South Tyrolese thus found themselves stuck, with lower average per capita incomes than the Italians,[6] and with nowhere to go for work except West Germany, since it was obviously unacceptable to undergo cultural assimilation in a town elsewhere in Italy. Protests at this situation by the SVP were contemptuously and deliberately ignored in Rome and Trento. The result was the start of terrorist activity, in 1956. Originally intended to draw attention to grievances, it was later organized by South Tyrolese to achieve separation from the Italian-dominated region, and then, after the arrest of its leaders, was taken over by Austrian pan-Germans and neo-nazis seeking the total separation of South Tyrol from Italy.

For its part the Austrian government, since 1955 fully independent and, significantly, with its borders fixed by Four-Power guarantee, raised the South Tyrol question at the United Nations in 1960 and 1961. Resolution 1497 (xv) urged Austria and Italy to start negotiations on 'all' aspects of the implementation of the 1946 Agreement. Until then, Italy had argued that the South Tyrol question was entirely an internal affair. This Resolution, coupled with the bombs of the terrorists, obliged the Italian government to begin discussions with the South Tyrolese on the

one hand, and Vienna on the other, with a view to improving the Regional Autonomy statute.

The result was the so-called Package Agreement of December 1969, basically negotiated between Bolzano and Rome, which gave very significant concessions to the South Tyrolese.[7] First, although the structure of the region was maintained, its main legislative powers were given to the provinces, so that the South Tyrolese were in a position to control the economic and social development of their homeland, and themselves. Second, the principle of ethnic proportionality in employment was to be strictly applied in all public bodies, including state and semi-state ones, and in all career grades, with the exception of the Ministries of the Interior and Defence. Third, all public officials had to be bilingual, with appointment and promotion requiring proof of language proficiency through examinations. Fourth, the provinces received substantial sources of revenue – in some cases up to 90 per cent of taxes raised in them as well as proportions of state sectoral expenditure in such matters as housing, roads and schools.

One result of the changes was that as the province of South Tyrol received more legislative powers, and the administrative powers of the region were automatically devolved, so the provincial civil service expanded.

The current situation

Twenty years later the province had been utterly transformed. In the 1990s commerce is thriving. The South Tyrolese, possessors of the land, have grown rich on CAP funds and the development of all-year tourism which has seen the Winter Olympics, the development of nine new ski areas, and provincial financial support for those wishing to modernize farms in order to take in tourists. There is considerable inward investment from Germany.

On the other hand, the position of the Italian community has deteriorated: with the new laws on ethnic proportionality in public employment, far fewer Italians can now get jobs in the administration; and the general recession of the 1970s led to the stagnation and even decline of the industrial sector. The Italian percentage of the provincial population fell from 34.3 per cent in 1961 to 27.65 per cent in 1991.[8] All these factors have resulted in a backlash led by the neo-fascist Movimento Sociale Italiano (MSI), which is, significantly, the largest Italian party on the Bolzano City Council, and openly calls for the abolition of the Autonomy Statute and the revocation of the concessions of the package.

South Tyrol as a European model

To what extent can South Tyrol be considered a valid model for other areas of Europe? This question will be considered under five headings: the overall Italian political system; power-sharing and decision-making in South Tyrol; the system of ethnic proportionality in public employment; the status of the minority language; and the question of self-determination.

The overall Italian political system

Italy is not a federal state but a regional one. This means that regions (and South Tyrol as an autonomous province more or less has regional powers) enjoy two types of legislative competence, primary and secondary. Under primary legislative competence regions may issue laws in regard to those matters laid down in their constitutions as long as they conform to the (national) constitution and the principles of the legal order of the state, respect international obligations and national interests (significantly, in the Trentino–Alto Adige region, these include the protection of local linguistic minorities), as well as the socioeconomic reforms of the Republic. Under secondary legislative competence, the regions (and South Tyrol) may issue laws in regard to a list of matters within the limits and principles of state laws. The problem with this system is that all laws passed by the regional and provincial legislature require approval and verification by the government in Rome, and most require also the adoption of so-called 'Executive Measures', decrees integrating the regional or provincial laws into the body of Italian national law, before they can come into effect. The vagueness of such phrases as 'respect for the socioeconomic reforms of the Republic' or 'national interests', as well as the legal complexities involved, provide much scope for conflict over definitions, legal disputes and delay, hence also an opportunity for those hostile to cultural minorities to exploit the situation. Certainly the South Tyrolese believe a federal system would be far more efficient, and they are leaders in the move for a Europe of the regions as opposed to a Europe of the states.

Power-sharing and decision-making

In South Tyrol power-sharing is institutionalized. That means the provincial government must be composed of representatives of the two main ethnic groups, in the ratio of 7 South Tyrolese to 3 Italians. This has not, so far, been difficult. After regional (including provincial) elections the SVP, which has always had a majority in the South Tyrol Assembly,

negotiates a common programme with like-minded Italian political parties. Since the SVP is part of the Christian Democratic family of European political parties, its usual partners are the Italian Christian Democrats and Social Democrats and even the Socialists. The danger in the system lies in what might happen if the Italian group came to be represented almost entirely by a party with an incompatible ideology. In the 1970s, for example, there was the possibility that the Communists would be in that position, and the SVP made it clear that it would not share power with them. Far more serious is the threat today that the Italian community might come to be dominated by the neo-fascist MSI. Clearly the SVP would not share power with a party whose political aim was the abolition of the South Tyrolese autonomy.

This highlights the issue of politico-territorial stability. The British and Irish governments have proposed power-sharing as a solution for Northern Ireland, but this has been resolutely rejected by the main unionist parties on the grounds that it is dishonest to require power-sharing when it is the intention of one of the parties sharing power to do away with the framework within which that power is shared. In the case of Cyprus, fears and uncertainty as to the territorial destiny of the island led to the failure of government based on institutional power-sharing between Greeks and Turks, amid mutual recrimination; this was followed by civil war, invasion, and the collapse of the Republic.

With regard to decision-making, in South Tyrol decisions are made by majority and there is nothing to prevent the majority SVP adopting legislation on its own. But apart from the need for legislation to be approved by Rome, if a bill is considered prejudicial to the equality of rights or cultural characteristics of a group, a majority of the deputies of that group can call for a vote by linguistic groups. If the bill is adopted despite two-thirds of the linguistic group in question voting against it, then the law may be contested before the Constitutional Court, but until decision by that latter body the law remains in effect. Similar provisions apply to the adoption of the regional and provincial budgets.[9]

In Cyprus, by contrast, the Greek and Turkish groups had the opportunity to veto certain legislation which they did not favour. The process of government soon broke down, particularly in regard to the levying and collecting of taxes, and soon afterwards the Republic collapsed.

Ethnic proportionality in public employment

Minorities are passionately devoted to their homeland, believing they have a right to live there. In this respect the London Declaration of June

1977, which recognized that the Palestinians had the right to a homeland, is surely of some significance. Minorities want a stake in their homeland; that is why issues of employment and housing are as vital as rights in regard to culture, education and language. The South Tyrolese sought to have a system of ethnic proportionality in order to overcome the legacy of fascism, when South Tyrolese were excluded from public employment on the grounds of the low quality of their Italian, and in order to ensure that their group participated in the administration of their homeland without having to compete for jobs against candidates from all over Italy.

However, to be effective such a system requires that persons declare officially to which ethnic or linguistic group they belong. In South Tyrol the system has caused some problems. What if people could not give the declaration, i.e. if they were the children of mixed marriages? What if people refused to give such a declaration on the grounds that it violated the equality of rights of all citizens without distinction as to sex, race, language, religion or political belief laid down in Article 3 of the Italian constitution? How would very small groups, such as the Ladins with 4 per cent of the population, be affected? What would happen if a group failed to fill its quota?

Indeed, as the Italian group realized that it would have to reduce its members in public employment (true ethnic proportions were to be achieved by the year 2002) and that there was little scope for employment in stagnating industry or South Tyrolese-dominated agri-tourism, it has been reported that some Italians have declared themselves or their children as German, and Italian children were being sent to German schools. Nothing could be done about this: in order to protect the South Tyrolese majority against a recurrence of fascist-type legislation, and in conformity with international precedent in the Judgment of the Permanent Court of International Justice of 26 April 1928 in regard to Upper Silesia, the legislation implementing the revised Autonomy Statute stipulated that declarations could not be verified or disputed by the authorities.[10]

However, one question that has arisen is whether a system of ethnic proportionality in public employment is compatible with the principle of freedom of movement stipulated in the Treaty of Rome. This basic freedom applies to member states of the European Union, and presumably would apply to other states if and when they joined. No person can be excluded from public appointment on grounds of nationality except in cases of the highest decision-making posts, the duties of which 'must

involve acts which affect private individuals by requiring their obedience or, in the event of disobedience, by compelling them to comply', and cases which could be claimed as specifically requiring loyalty as a factor for consideration, such as the armed forces, the security services, the judiciary, and taxation authorities.[11] But the question of ethnic proportionality hides another issue, which is highlighted elsewhere in this book. Ethnic proportionality is a group right. Minorities usually want group rights, but human rights are concerned with the individual. The clash between ethnic proportionality in public employment in South Tyrol and the freedom of movement stipulated by the European Union reflects that conflict between group and individual rights.

The status of the minority language

In many countries minority languages are official, at least locally. But the German language in South Tyrol is not an official language. Under the De Gasperi–Gruber Agreement German was 'parified' with Italian in the region. But when the South Tyrolese argued that this meant German was or should be an official language, the Council of State ruled in 1952 that Italy was under no obligation to make it official since if the negotiators of the Agreement had meant it to be official, they would have said so unequivocally. The situation did not alter under the improved Autonomy Statute.

Language has been described as the last bastion of defence of a minority's homeland, in that language qualifications or knowledge might be required for employment. But to what extent can language any longer be called a defence in the European Union, particularly against freedom of movement? The European Court of Justice has ruled that if the Treaty of Rome did not prohibit a policy for the protection and promotion of national or official languages,

> the implementation of such a policy must not encroach upon a fundamental freedom such as that of the free movement of workers. Therefore the requirements deriving from measures intended to implement such a policy must not in any circumstances be disproportionate in relation to the aim pursued, and the manner in which they are applied must not bring about discrimination against nationals of other Member States.

Ambiguous though this is about the requirement to know an official language, the implication is that the requirement to know a non-official

language might be ruled an infringement of the Treaty of Rome.[12] The South Tyrol system of ethnic proportionality and bilingualism in public employment can therefore be considered to be under threat, and the way open, via freedom of movement, to changes in the ethnic composition of the province. It is to be noted that a recent Italian law designed to defend minority languages and cultures nowhere states that these languages are official,[13] and even in Britain the recent Welsh language bill has been criticized on the grounds that even if Welsh were to have 'equal standing' with English in public business and justice, nevertheless it was still not an official language in the Principality.[14]

Self-determination

Finally, the South Tyrol question raised the issue of self-determination. The problem for the SVP was how to argue that self-determination was an inalienable right of the South Tyrolese ethnic group and still reconcile this with the political necessity of operating legally within the Italian state. There were two problems: first, the association of self-determination with secession, which was likely to arouse the hostility of the majority; and, second, the question of whether one could apply to ethnic groups a principle which is accepted for whole peoples. A solution was developed by Professor Theodore Veiter, who interpreted the principle of self-determination as meaning the right of a people or group to decide freely what legislative and administrative powers might be necessary in the cultural and possibly other fields in order to enable it to maintain its cultural characteristics and separate identity, and to demand these from the host state. Separation would be sought only as a last resort if legitimate demands were denied.[15]

To criticisms that the South Tyrol autonomy has created a situation of apartheid, the South Tyrolese reply that their experiences at the hands of the Fascists and during the early years of postwar democratic Italy gave rise to defensive strategies. Italians may have suffered under fascism, but their national identity and cultural characteristics were never threatened. Ever since the De Gasperi–Gruber Agreement, the South Tyrolese have never tired of pointing out that protection of minorities is an ongoing process; that changes in politics, society and technology may well require changes in existing institutions and constitutions; and therefore that calls for dialogue and debate about change should not be seen as treason, or as an insatiable demand for more. In this respect at least, the South Tyrol experience is valid for all European minorities.

Notes

1 Südtiroler Volkspartei, 'Konvention über die Grundrechte der Europäischen Volksgruppen', Bolzano/Bozen, May 1991, submitted to the CSCE Conference of Experts on National Minorities, Geneva, July 1991.

2 A.E. Alcock, *History of the South Tyrol Question* (London: Michael Joseph, 1970), pp. 139–40.

3 Constitutional Law of 2 February 1948.

4 Alcock, op. cit., pp. 205–6 and 285–6.

5 Ibid., p. 276.

6 An average disparity of 20 per cent. Alcock, op. cit., p. 265.

7 The full details in ibid., pp. 434–49.

8 'Autonome Provinz Bozen-Südtirol', *Südtirol-Handbuch 1988* (ed) Table 8, p. 180, Bolzano, 1989; *Volksbote* (Bolzano), 11 June 1992.

9 Decree of the President of the Republic, 31 August 1972, no. 60, Arts 56 and 84.

10 The issue of ethnic proportions in public employment is examined in greater depth in A.E. Alcock, 'Proportional representation in public employment as a technique for diminishing conflict in culturally divided communities – the case of South Tyrol', in *Regional Politics and Policy* (London: Cass, 1991), vol. 1, no. 1, pp. 74–86.

11 This issue is examined in greater depth in A.E. Alcock, 'The protection of regional cultural minorities and the process of European integration: the example of South Tyrol', in *International Relations*, vol. XI, 1992, no. 1, pp. 17–36.

12 Ibid.

13 Law no. 612 of 20 November 1991.

14 *Daily Telegraph*, 19 December 1992 and 20 January 1993.

15 Theodore Veiter, *Das Menschenrecht*, Vienna, April 1970, p. 12.

6

THE FORMER YUGOSLAVIA

ZORAN PAJIC

As recently as 1990, as Yugoslavia headed towards its first multi-party elections, all options seemed open. Yugoslavia was first on the waiting-list to join the Council of Europe, and relations with the European Community were improving. Moves towards market-oriented economic reforms and privatization were beginning to show significant results.

But the federal political structures could no longer hold; the Communist Party establishment was in a state of panic, and the indoctrinated Yugoslav People's Army (JNA) was in total confusion over how to adapt to the changes and the imminent loss of its privileged position. It was obvious that despite a common Communist Party and ideological background, the leaders of the six republics could forge no political consensus on issues that were crucial for the future of the country.

Nor did the global changes in the international community give much hope for the continued stability of Yugoslavia. The fall of the Berlin Wall symbolized the beginning of a new era in which there is no role for the country 'between East and West', a role which Yugoslavia had played so well for forty years. The non-aligned movement, another trade mark of Yugoslavia's world image, was facing increasing marginalization in international relations. These developments had a very strong and disturbing impact on the people, highlighting frustrations and the feeling of betrayal. At least two generations of Yugoslavs had been spoiled by their country's postwar role: bridging the Iron Curtain, leading the non-aligned countries, experimenting with the self-management system, successfully combining communist rule with some individual freedoms unknown under that system (the freedom to travel abroad, to hold private property, to keep a hard-currency bank account, to emigrate and to

return). In the divided Cold War world, Yugoslavs believed they were something special.

At the domestic level, Yugoslavia offered the great majority of people a predictable life, with the feeling of being taken care of by the 'system'. They used to follow the same pattern of protected careers and well-planned futures. Tuition from nursery school through to university level was free, jobs were easily available (at least until the 1980s), as a rule housing was provided by the state, health care was free, and pensions were guaranteed.

It is true that the system encouraged a general mediocrity as a way of life. But this stable stagnation was a very comfortable environment for ordinary people, happy with the average, protected from changes and challenges. This philosophy can be illustrated by the popular saying: 'We pretend to work, and the state pretends to pay us.' This was the way Yugoslavs explained their system and its safe durability.

The enormous changes on the global political and economic level, beginning especially in the late 1980s, required a dramatic alteration in this mentality. And when the change came, it caught Yugoslavia by surprise. The old ideology, good or bad – there is little point in evaluating it now – disappeared almost overnight, but new values had not yet been created. This tremendous psychological void had to be filled in one way or another.

In comparison with the previous way of life, the future offered by the reform-minded political parties was quite terrifying. Their standard election messages included phrases such as 'open market economy', 'competition', and 'the struggle to achieve European standards'. People were simply not ready for such a vision. The institutions of a civil society could have played a role in soothing people's fears of an unknown future and in solving conflicts, but they were virtually non-existent. One might argue that after so many years of comfortable collective identity within the system, the average Yugoslav was simply unprepared to take responsibility to exercise individual freedom.

The easiest option was therefore to seek another form of collective identity, another protective shield against the confusion. This was nationalism. Many politicians quickly realized that the nationalist ticket was a life-line for them too. It could be used as a tool to homogenize people and to create the constituency that, in the one-party system, they had never had.

In this context it is also important to note Yugoslavia's lack of democratic experience in conflict resolution. During Marshal Tito's regime,

social conflicts were resolved by two means: the more or less indisputable authority of the Communist Party, and the personalized role of Tito as the supreme arbiter. Disputes were settled behind the scenes, by political pressure in pre-arranged party meetings. From the outside, one could form the impression that Yugoslavia was almost a society without conflicts. The truth was that they were merely contained. With Tito's death in 1980 and the collapse of the Party, conflicts started exploding everywhere, but no democratic structures, institutions or procedures had been developed to manage them and to offer a peaceful way out of the crisis.

These factors provide the context for a better understanding of the pre-election period throughout Yugoslavia and the subsequent disaster in the region. Once the nationalist parties with their hardline ideologies had been elected, conflict, especially in Bosnia and Herzegovina, became all but inevitable. After more than two years of the devastating war in the Balkans, it is apparent that democratic governments in western Europe and elsewhere do not understand nationalism as another form of totalitarianism and authoritarianism, as well as the crucial factor in the hostilities. Former communist politicians (Milosevic, Tudjman) and nationalistic newcomers (Karadzic, Boban) used it as a pragmatic political option to exploit both the ideological vacuum and people's profound sense of personal insecurity. This provides a far more precise and concrete explanation for the divisive politics than any reference to historical animosities.

Bosnia and Herzegovina

In any attempt to understand the new reality of ethnic majority and minority situations, the case of Bosnia and Herzegovina is of particular interest. By getting the green light from the European Community for the effective partition of Bosnia and Herzegovina along ethnic lines,* all three nationalist parties† achieved their long-term strategic aims. Long before the war, which 'officially' started on 6 April 1992, these parties had heightened the sense of fear and mistrust among different ethnic groups by blaming 'the others' for their own 'oppressed history and misery'. This was followed by chauvinistic statements by politicians and

* A Statement of Principles for the New Constitutional Settlement of Bosnia and Herzegovina was issued at an EC-sponsored conference in Lisbon on 18 March 1992.

† HDZ – Hrvatska Demokratska Zajednica, the Croat party led by Mate Boban; SDA – Straka Demokratska Akcije, the Muslim party led by Alija Izetbegovic; and SDS – Srbska Demokratska Stranka, the Serb party led by Radovan Karadzic.

loyal intellectuals and finally by tolerating terrorism and encouraging the illegal stockpiling of arms. Frightened, lonely individuals – lacking civil and legal protection, and financially squeezed – were offered the shelter of collective rights.

These developments are the logical outcome of the rise of rival nationalist leaders in a multi-ethnic community such as Bosnia and Herzegovina was (it was often labelled 'Little Yugoslavia' because of its ethnic and religious diversity). It was naive to believe that three nationalist leaders could coexist within a single state. As a rule, all nationalist leaders dream of being in control of their own nation-territory; of establishing their own legal order and economy; of having their own military and police, etc. These are the instruments by which they transform themselves from leaders to heads of state. This is not unique to the Yugoslav situation, although its Yugoslav manifestation is one of the deadliest. Throughout the world hundreds of different ethnic groups are struggling for statehood under a banner declaring 'We can't live together with...'; all of them want a state to call their own, or at least to see their (ethnic, tribal) government ruling an autonomous province, if not an independent state.

Preparations for the ethnic division of Bosnia and Herzegovina have not happened quickly because it has not been easy to persuade ordinary citizens to see that their friends, neighbours, or even relatives belong on the other side of the barricade. But eventually the nationalist propaganda war which began between Serbia and Croatia spread to Bosnia and Herzegovina too. There, too, people's perceptions of one another have been reduced to primitive stereotypes of Serb, Muslim and Croat zealots. The Belgrade media would refer to Croats as 'Ustashi', Zagreb would call Serbs 'Chetnik', and both would portray Muslims as 'filthy fundamentalists'. The aim of this ferocious and warmongering propaganda was, and still is, to ease the conscience of people, to allow them to hate and ultimately to throw themselves into an atrocious war.

Even before the war started, the nationalists were indiscriminate in the means they chose to achieve their ultimate goal of creating ethnic states. They frantically tried to compromise Radio and TV Sarajevo and the daily newspaper *Oslobodjenje*. They relentlessly pressured the schools to accept religious education curricula and to classify teachers and headmasters of schools on the basis of their national party membership. The only obstacle they faced was the considerable number of 'unreliable and suspicious' people who lived together peaceably in ethnically mixed communities.

Although important differences existed among national parties in Bosnia and Herzegovina, there is no doubt that their respective political projects would have brought them to the same end – extreme national homogenization. The political and psychological environment that fostered the concepts underlying the Lisbon Statement was created very skilfully. The ruling political parties had accustomed the people to believe that their leaders could not agree on anything and that if they did not agree they would have to wage war. Such a belief meant that people were prepared to accept anything – even a very problematic and risky settlement – that avoided serious troubles. It seems that today many tend to forget that the European Community put all its diplomatic support behind the project of ethnically clean territories in Bosnia and Herzegovina – still the major political 'vision' that Europe is able to offer to the region! This is the core political issue and remains the only option on the agenda of the UN–EU International Conference on the Former Yugoslavia in Geneva. It is based on the principle of 'divide and quit', which has been tried before in some other crisis areas (Cyprus, India–Pakistan, Palestine) but has never worked as a viable long-term solution.

It is clear that in the case of Bosnia, with its ethnically interwoven experience and cosmopolitan cities, this partition plan is a euphemism for an apartheid system, based as it is on the total segregation of ethnic groups. While apartheid is falling apart in South Africa, it is being reborn in southern Europe. The logic of the Lisbon Statement and its subsequent elaboration correspond perfectly to the idea of a regime in which every individual has a precisely determined place in society from the cradle to the grave. A person's domicile, the type of education one is entitled to, as well as the conditions for intimate relations, are determined on the basis of race, or, to use the language adopted by the Lisbon declaration, on the basis of 'national principle'. The idea was to achieve the separate development of different ethnic groups and to discourage or even ban any coexistence. Once isolation was achieved, nationalistic propaganda would become much easier to believe and people would accept such a system as the best solution for all.

For an objective analyst it was clear that from the day ethnic territories or states ('statelets' is the most recent jargon) within Bosnia were proclaimed, individuals from all three 'genuine' nations (Serbs, Muslims and Croats, throughout Bosnian history) would find themselves in a 'dual' situation, depending on their locations. In an entity where an individual is part of the majority nationality, he or she would enjoy the status of full citizenship, with guarantees of full civil and political rights.

Meanwhile, a person of the same ethnicity, by the mere fact of being in a province where another nation has a majority, would become a second-class citizen. Even this absurd outcome seemed acceptable for the majority of voters who endorsed their own ethnic parties, as well as for the European Community. This attitude could be understood as a choice between two evils: war or ethnic partition. The international community underestimated the philosophy of nationalism and the idea of ethnic exclusivity. And it totally overlooked the reality of the Bosnian demographic map (i.e. the mixed communities, the regions never before defined according to ethnic criteria, the large number of 'national atheists') which, if read carefully, could give it the clear message that the type of partition it had in mind inevitably involved massive displacement of the population and the redrawing of municipal boundaries.

The crucial conclusion to be drawn is this: in Bosnia and Herzegovina it is not possible to rewrite history without war. Indeed, the agreement on 'cantonization based on the national principle', signed in Lisbon by Izetbegovic, Karadzic and Boban, under the chairmanship of Ambassador Cutillero, collapsed only two weeks later. Or it may be more accurate to say that its implementation started with the first wave of ethnic cleansing carried out by Serb paramilitary forces and by their shelling and later siege of Sarajevo in April 1992. Karadzic played the first card because he was much better prepared and felt very confident with the full backing of the JNA and the regime in Belgrade. Almost two years after this overture, there is no doubt that the lack of political will among democratic governments to understand the substance of Balkan-style nationalistic policies encouraged the architects of Greater Serbia and subsequently of Greater Croatia, and finally endorsed the attempt by radicals among the Muslim population to seek their own piece of 'ethnic land'.

All this has happened at the expense of ordinary people who, by pure chance, happened to be born as Muslims, Croats or Serbs, but who have been killed, displaced, raped, 'ethnically cleansed', and humiliated only because of their ethnic origin. The peoples of the former Yugoslavia have become bearers of the collective guilt for the atrocities committed by relatively few among them. A generation of well-educated, committed Europeans from Bosnia has been sacrificed either through physical elimination or through exile. Those who believed in tolerance and pluralism as a normal way of life were labelled as unreliable by the ethnic leaders and finally were left with no country to turn to as their own. Those who stayed or found shelter in besieged towns and 'safe areas' have became a strong card in the deadly poker game of power politics.

Sarajevo has been under siege since April 1992; Mostar has been destroyed in the effort to divide it. It is here that the destruction of pluralism shows its ugliest face. For those who not only experienced but literally lived the extraordinary Bosnian amalgam of different cultures, religions, nations, mentalities, architects and customs, the 'unbearable lightness of destruction' of all human values that the democratic world has stood for is totally incomprehensible.

Ethnic constitutionalism

This political, psychological and warmongering background represents the stage on which minorities are bound to play their role in the new 'ethnic constitutionalism' in the countries which emerged from the former Yugoslavia. I have deliberately excluded the 'legal background' from this description, because of my deep scepticism about the 'normative haven' supposedly found in the Yugoslav constitutional tradition. The federal constitution, as well as those of the constituent republics, was formulated in statements giving an idealized picture of the society and the political regime. This was remarkably well elaborated in the sections dealing with human rights, which expressed a strong political commitment to all three 'generations' of human rights.

In reality, human rights issues very much reflected fluctuating political trends within the leadership of the Communist Party, over more than 40 years. Throughout this period, tolerance and a relaxed attitude towards minorities tended to prevail. Although the very progressive and generous legal provisions in this area were not decisive for the social environment, they did contribute to Yugoslavia's excellent reputation for the treatment of minorities. The constitutional guarantees for the safeguarding of minority identity were substantial and comprehensive. The protection of the native language of minority groups in the former Yugoslavia will remain unrivalled in constitutional practice for a long time; minority languages were widely used in the minorities' own printed and electronic media, in schools, in higher education (including at the university for the Albanian minority in Pristina, Kosovo), in cultural and art societies, on public signposts and in public administration. There was, in fact, only one area in which they were excluded and Serbo-Croat was the only official language – the army. And, of course, there was one area in which minorities could not perform as distinctive ethnic groups – in the formation of political parties. This prohibition, however, applied to all entities in the former Yugoslavia, because the

Communist Party had a monopoly over the political infrastructure.

In spite of its attempt at total control, the Party never abandoned the 'programme' of coexistence of different ethnic groups, very often ignoring the criteria of 'majority' or 'minority'. In principle, the 1974 constitution treats both 'nations' and 'nationalities' equally. The Socialist Federal Republic of Yugoslavia defined Yugoslavia both as a federal state and as a community. The federation consisted of 'voluntary united nations and their socialist republics and the autonomous provinces of Vojvodina and Kosovo, which are constituent parts of the Socialist Republic of Serbia'. The community was defined as an alliance 'of working people and citizens and of nations and nationalities having equal rights'. This vocabulary may seem awkward but was very common in the Yugoslav legislation, which very often translated common terms (such as minority, people) into more appropriate, politically correct terminology. The word 'minority' was officially considered offensive and pejorative and, by a stroke of pen, was transformed into 'nationality'. Similarly, the expression 'working people' was considered in the early stages of communism in Yugoslavia to be a 'vanguard' and the 'base' for the development of socialism, in contrast to the term 'citizens', which stood for all the population. The wording of Article 1 of the constitution was a compromise which left a number of questions open and finally led to tensions. Two issues of crucial importance were highlighted by the first attempts at ethnic homogenization. The first stumbling-block, which produced much of the later violence and war in the region, was the status of the Serbian population in Croatia, after it became clear that this republic was heading towards independence. The second was crystallized in the question: 'To which nation did Bosnia and Herzegovina belong?' From the beginning of 1990, political movements and parties sprang up both in Serbia and in Croatia, respectively claiming large parts of Bosnia and Herzegovina for their own nation. The predominant reaction in Bosnia and Herzegovina was that it did not belong to any of its nations (Serbs, Croats or Muslims), but to its inhabitants ('working people and citizens').

Throughout the world, the fall of communism has gone hand in hand with the revival of nationalism, which is very often transformed into chauvinism, exclusivity and militant extremism. This tendency is reflected in most post-communist constitutions by a very narrow and exclusive definition of the state. The 'strategic ideal' of 'ethnic revival' is being translated into a pragmatic call for 'one state for every ethnic group'. The case of former Yugoslavia can be taken as a paradigm of this

phenomenon. The states which emerged from it seem to be 'constitutionally owned' by the relevant nation, while the presence of members of other ethnic groups is considered to be an anomaly and a burden inherited from the past. Even if they do not advocate the expulsion or 'exchange' of population (as in the case of Bosnia and Herzegovina), nationalist leaders pledge only to tolerate the presence of these other ethnic groups.

The prevailing rhetoric in the respective constitutions of Croatia, Serbia and Slovenia is often a compromise between theoretical confusion and an attempt to make it clear beyond any doubt that the state 'belongs' to the given nation.

The wording of the 1990 constitution of the Republic of *Croatia* reflects the ideal of a nation-state:

> The Republic of Croatia is established as a national state of the
> Croat nation and a state of members of other nations and minorities,
> who are its citizens: Serbs, Muslims, Slovenes, Czechs, Slovaks,
> Italians, Hungarians, Jews and others...

It should be noted that this chapter (I) of the constitution contains a brief history of the Croats from the seventh century to the present day. This historical saga reads as a vindication of continuous Croat statehood, irrespective of long periods of consociation with others in wider, pluralistic entities.

According to the preamble of its 1990 constitution, *Serbia* is

> a democratic state of the Serbian people in which members of other
> nations and national minorities will be able to exercise their na-
> tional rights...

In addition, one finds a strong emphasis on the 'freedom-loving, democratic, and state-building traditions of the Serbian people'.

The preamble of the constitution of the Republic of *Slovenia* (1991) explains the state as an entity stemming from

> the basic and permanent right of the Slovene nation to self-
> determination and from the historical fact that the Slovenes have
> formed, over many centuries of struggle for national liberation,
> their own national identity and established their own statehood.

The result is an ambiguous compromise, as stated in Article 3:

> Slovenia is a state of all citizens, based on the permanent and
> inviolable right of the Slovene nation to self-determination.

Conclusion

The process of consolidation of the new states is still in its initial stages, and it would not be fair to draw firm conclusions one way or the other, in particular for those countries which are still at war. Nevertheless, the tendency towards an ethnically 'pure' state is very noticeable. The common starting-point in most of the 'new and democratic' constitutions is the idea that the *raison d'être of the state is to serve the nation and its citizens*. This leaves little room for individual rights. An individual is treated as a member of a group, and rights and freedoms are granted and guaranteed on that basis only. If an individual belongs to a small group that cannot qualify as a 'national minority', there is very little possibility of claiming rights as a citizen only. Even worse, there are cases where an individual would refuse to be classified as a member of a group for various reasons (mixed ethnic background is very common among Yugoslavs, there are many cases of intermarriage, and many who dissent from the 'national' leaders and would therefore be reluctant to declare their ethnic background). The state, as the constitutional provisions quoted above suggest, is in the first place owned by the 'host' ethnic group and in the second place may be regarded as a home for people who qualify as members of a recognized minority ethnic group, and who are treated as 'historical guests'. Thus any individual who does not belong to a recognized group does not belong anywhere.

7

THE REST OF THE BALKANS*

HUGH POULTON

Introduction

Despite Greece's claim of continuity from ancient Greece, and Bulgaria's claim to 1,300 years of existence, none of the Balkan states date from earlier than the nineteenth century. The entire area was part of the Ottoman empire for centuries. This Ottoman heritage – especially the *millet* system, whereby the population was clearly differentiated by religious affiliation – as well as geographical factors, resulted in compartmentalized communities. Since the Ottoman empire did not attempt to assimilate Christian or Jewish minorities, the peoples of the Balkans managed to retain their separate identities and cultures. Many of them also retained a sense of a glorious history when they controlled a particular area, often at the expense of their neighbours who likewise made (and still make) historical claims to the territory in question.

The disintegration of the Ottoman empire in the Balkans led to the emergence of small states at the periphery – initially Serbia in the north and Greece in the south but later Romania and Bulgaria as well. All of them followed policies of aggressive expansion to enlarge themselves and to bring their perceived fellow nationals into the new national states. This expansion or enosis was initially at the expense of the decaying Ottoman empire, but by the early twentieth century states were competing directly for some regions – most notably Macedonia. The exception was Albania, which arrived late in the race because the majority of the population shared their rulers' Muslim religion. They were thus less susceptible to influence by the new creed of nationalism, or by outside Western (Christian) benefactors.

* This chapter deals with minority rights in Albania, Bulgaria, Greece, Kosovo and Macedonia.

66

Consequently the new states were perceived as ethnic states based on one dominant nation. They suffered from irredentism on the one hand, and internal tensions between majority and minority communities on the other. These crucial problems have remained. In addition the relative 'newness' of these states, their turbulent history of internecine wars with neighbours, and the expansion and contraction of their borders, contribute to enduring feelings of insecurity. This is most evident in Greece's reactions to an independent Macedonia.

The interwar period
The provisions relating to minorities in the various treaties which recognized the post-First World War states in the Balkans concentrated on civil and political rights. Common to all the treaties were provisions that all citizens should be treated equally before the law regardless of race, language and religion; that minorities should have the right to establish (at their own expense) social, religious and charitable institutions and schools with free use of mother tongue and religion; and that in areas of minority concentration, mother-tongue education should be provided in primary schools alongside the official language instruction, and minority languages should be recognized in legal courts. In practice these remained on the whole merely paper provisions and were often flagrantly ignored, with little attempt by the international community at making states comply.

In the Kingdom of Serbs, Croats and Slovenes (later called *Yugoslavia*), Serbian was compulsory in schools and for official purposes in both Macedonia (referred to as South Serbia) and Kosovo. The Macedonians (or Bulgarians) were not recognized and an attempt at Serbianization of the population took place. In Kosovo, irregular Serbian troops, the Chetniks, were formed to keep the majority Albanian population down, and an estimated 40,000 Orthodox Slav peasants (mostly Serbs/Montenegrins) were moved in and given good land and benefits, while over half a million ethnic Albanians were forced to emigrate from the region.

In *Greece* in 1925 the government announced that it would no longer follow the 1924 protocol (which had placed the Bulgarian minority there under League of Nations protection) and would henceforth consider its Slav minorities to be ethnically Greek. Following this all Slavonic place names were changed to Greek ones. Massive population exchanges with Turkey (in 1924) and to a lesser extent with Bulgaria (in 1919) had seen huge numbers of immigrant Greeks settled in minority areas in the north.

The state pursued an active, often repressive assimilation policy which, with the exception of the Muslim Turkish minority of Western Thrace (exempted from these mass exchanges by the Treaty of Lausanne), was relatively successful.

Albania remained politically weak. Barely a functioning state, it increasingly fell under Italian control, which made assessment of its minority policies problematic.

In *Bulgaria* there was a continuation of the noticeable large-scale emigration of ethnic Turks and other Muslims which had been encouraged by the authorities from the outset of the modern state. Turkish schools, especially primary schools, were closed. The advent of dictatorship in 1934 saw a further deterioration, with a ban on the use of the new Latin script and the reinstatement of the Arabic script for all Turkish publications and classes. This was an apparent attempt both to dissuade mother-tongue expression and to hinder links with Ataturk's Turkey.

The communist period

Greece, the one non-communist Balkan country, continued its apparently deliberate confusion of citizenship, ethnicity and religion by its policy of denying virtually all minority rights – even to the extent of refusing to recognize that there were minorities other than 'Muslim' ones in the country. The Greek example contradicts the view that the explosion of nationalist forces in eastern Europe and the Balkans is a by-product of the collapse of communism. Certainly nationalism has filled the power vacuum following the demise of the discredited former ideology of Marxism-Leninism, but the threat of destructive nationalism is ever-present in the Balkans without necessarily having to feed on decaying communist systems.

The other countries which were pursuing different brands of communism in this period displayed divergent minority policies. In *Bulgaria* the Zhivkov regime over a long period pursued a repressive forced assimilation policy which was progressively applied to all the country's significant minority populations with the exception, for propaganda reasons, of the small Jewish and Armenian ones. This policy came to a head with the massive violent campaign against the ethnic Turkish minority – some 10 per cent of the population – in late 1984.

In *Albania*, by contrast, the Hoxha regime, while pursuing a policy of extreme denial of individual human rights, diverged from the Greek and Bulgarian models in allowing educational and cultural rights to its mi-

norities. However, the attempt at eradicating organized religion adversely affected minorities like the Greek one in the south, part of whose self-identification is bound up with Orthodox Christianity. There were also other measures relating to names, and reports of *de facto* restrictions on the use of the Greek language in some settings. Thus although the Hoxha regime did not pursue such an open assimilatory policy as Bulgaria or Greece, it did undercut some of the fundamental bases of minority identity by its harsh policies, its fervent Albanian nationalism and its attempts to unify the country, as well as its rigid ideological standpoints.

Tito's *Yugoslavia*, which became known as the Socialist Federal Republic of Yugoslavia (SFRJ), was the least homogeneous European state. It evolved a multinational federation based on a complicated three-tier system of national rights that was entrenched in the 1974 constitution. At the top were the six 'nations of Yugoslavia',* each with a national 'home' based in one of the republics – thus the Albanians of Kosovo, despite their numerical superiority over Montenegrins and others, were denied republican status because their national 'home' was outside Yugoslavia. Below those came the 'nationalities of Yugoslavia', which were legally entitled to cultural and linguistic rights. The largest group was the Albanians, concentrated in Kosovo and Western Macedonia. The lowest category was 'other nationalities and ethnic groups'.

From its inception in the Second World War, communist Yugoslavia recognized a separate Macedonian people who were one of the 'nations of Yugoslavia', and the postwar state actively and aggressively encouraged the cementing of a Macedonian national consciousness. As such, the Macedonians for the first time achieved considerable group benefits, albeit within the communist system. The ethnic Albanians of Macedonia – who make up over 20 per cent of the new republic's population and are concentrated in areas in the west where they formed majorities – were, in classic Balkan fashion, seen as a potential threat to the now dominant Macedonians. Even though the system granted educational and cultural facilities to Albanians and other minority groups, distrust between the two communities was deep, and any form of Albanian nationalistic activity was heavily penalized – in fact throughout the 1980s penal policy against Albanian nationalists was heavier in Macedonia than in Kosovo. In key institutions like the League of Communists, the percentage of Macedonians was disproportionately high.

* Bosnia and Herzegovina, Croatia, Macedonia, Montenegro, Serbia and Slovenia.

The 1974 constitution recognized Kosovo as an autonomous province of the republic of Serbia. This was the end-product of a process of granting greater group rights to Kosovo Albanians after the fall of Aleksander Rankovic, the Serb head of the security forces, in 1966. The constitution stressed the rights of 'working people' and 'the nationalities' rather than 'the citizen' or 'the individual', and there was a duality between rights for state power and for 'self-management associations of people'. While republican rights were those deriving from state powers, the rights of the autonomous provinces of Kosovo and Vojvodina were relegated to the level of 'self-management' rights; actually, however, both provinces had *de facto* republican rights. The rise of Slobodan Milosevic in the late 1980s was intimately connected with the growth of aggrieved Serbian nationalism both over the perceived threat to Serbs in Kosovo, and over the anomalies of Kosovo and Vojvodina as 'republics within a republic'. Serbia effectively destroyed the 1974 set-up, and the ethnic Albanians of Kosovo were progressively stripped of all autonomy. It should be remembered that in Kosovo – even at the best period for collective rights for Kosovo Albanians – and in Macedonia (as elsewhere in former Yugoslavia, with the possible exception of Slovenia), basic individual human rights like freedom of expression were never recognized and respected.

Thus the situations of minorities varied greatly from country to country. With Bulgaria and Greece members of opposing military systems (the Warsaw Pact and NATO respectively), Yugoslavia a leading member of the non-aligned movement, and Albania deliberately in almost total isolation, the opportunities for transnational systems of minority protection were few. In the area of international protection, all the Balkan countries except Albania had ratified the various international agreements such as the International Covenant on Civil and Political Rights (ICCPR), Article 27 of which guarantees minority rights. Nevertheless there was little censure of repressive actions.

Even though Greece, as an EC member, was potentially susceptible to pressure, it was viewed as a vital outpost of NATO and the West, and thus its restrictive internal minority policies were scarcely criticized. Similarly, the West saw a 'non-aligned' Yugoslavia as preferable to the country falling again into the Soviet camp, and under Tito it was allowed to run up massive debts. When the situation in Kosovo exploded in 1981 with subsequent large-scale human rights abuses which continued throughout the decade, there was little international interest or censure. There was a similar reaction when the Milosevic regime removed all

autonomy from the province and put it under naked military/police occupation. In the same way, even when Zhivkov's Bulgaria embarked on its extraordinary campaign against the ethnic Turks little real action was taken.

One of the most effective ways of applying international pressure was through the UN procedure for confidentially reviewing communications about human rights violations. Even Albania has been made to answer allegations of human rights abuses under UN Resolution 1503/728F (the so-called '1503 procedure'). However, when Amnesty International submitted major complaints under this procedure about the forced assimilation campaign in Bulgaria, in June 1986 and again in May 1987, they were not taken up. Nevertheless, the drastically changed international climate after the sweeping changes in 1989 transformed the situation, opening up new possibilities and threats. The rest of this chapter considers the current position of minorities in the various parts of this region.

Kosovo

The situation in Kosovo remains acutely problematic and may easily ignite an international conflict. The stripping of autonomy from the province has been accompanied by the almost total exclusion of the Kosovo Albanians from power and decision-making, and the Belgrade authorities have pursued a relentless policy of centralization. The Albanians have responded by peaceful resistance, forming underground structures for both government and education, and have so far displayed a remarkable sense of unity as well as a commendable insistence on non-violence. How long this can last is debatable, especially given the open presence of Serb paramilitary organizations associated with Vojislav Seselj's Serbian Radical Party as well as extremists like Zelko Razjatovic ('Arkan').

In July 1992, the authorities set up a Federal Ministry of Human and Minority Rights with provincial branches. Its viewpoint is amply illustrated by the draft declaration of 23 November 1992 regarding Kosovo, which declared that all minority rights of Kosovo Albanians were secured but that 'the results of the ethnic cleansing by Albanian secessionists were being used in international relations as one of the primary means to exert pressure on the Republic of Serbia'.[r] Many of the articles in the constitution relating to inter-communal issues, e.g. linguistic rights, are left deliberately vague: rights are to be 'in accordance with the law'. The impression (strengthened by an obvious error in the wording of

Article 14 which has not even been corrected) is that the current document, like previous constitutions of the communist period, is a constitution in name only.

The international efforts in former Yugoslavia began on 7 July 1991 with the Brioni Accords, more than two years after the Serbian constitutional changes which had stripped Kosovo of its autonomy. The Hague Conference which began in September 1991 had eight representatives from former Yugoslavia, with Serbs as delegates for Kosovo (as well as Vojvodina). The Kosovo Albanians were willing to take part but at that time the principle was to deal only with republics. At the beginning of October 1991 a working group was set up which met with the Kosovo Albanians and fed back both to the EC and to the Serbian delegates. Repeated efforts to hold trilateral talks between Serbs, Kosovo Albanians and the EC failed because the Serbs refused to allow outsiders (i.e. the EC) to be present for what they considered to be an internal matter, and the Kosovo Albanians refused to talk without them. This impasse lasted until the London conference held in August 1992.

A main stumbling-block remains the education question. Kosovo Albanians set up a parallel underground education system after the Serbian authorities introduced a new curriculum. Currently some 320,000 primary school pupils and 90,000 secondary school pupils are being educated in these underground private schools. The chief difference is that the Kosovo Albanians want to reopen education on all three levels without conditions and then negotiate, while the Serb authorities want the problems of the teaching programmes and personnel, and the issue of time spent in parallel underground education institutions, discussed and assessed before reopening the system. Deadlock continues.

The Working Group on Ethnic and National Communities, under Ambassador Geert Ahrens, set up on 3 September 1992 for the International Conference on the former Yugoslavia in Geneva, worked out an autonomy solution for Kosovo based on the 1974 constitution and the experience of South Tyrol, Spain, the Åland Islands, Bosnia-Herzegovina and Croatia. Clearly some form of autonomy for Kosovo is essential. But it was not thought advisable to try to impose a solution. If and when the Kosovo Albanians do gain any form of autonomy, the question of how they would treat minorities within Kosovo will arise. A hopeful sign is that after the May 1992 clandestine elections, 14 seats of the underground parliament were kept open for Serb and Montenegrin members – who of course did not take part – under the proportional representation system used. Also the Kosovo Albanians claimed that it

was in Kosovo under the then Kosovo Albanian administration that the breakthrough in Roma (gypsy) media occurred.

A CSCE mission was resident in Kosovo from September 1992 until July 1993, when the Serbian government refused to allow its work to continue. The main task of this mission was not to propose settlements on constitutional issues like independence, autonomy or unification, nor was the primary aim to observe and monitor, although of course it did do this. The overriding aim was to try to prevent armed conflict from spreading to Kosovo. The mission operated in a buffer capacity. The monitors were not prosecutors, investigators or judges, but tried to be impartial and keep reasonable relations with all parties, whether governments, police, army or ethnic groups. The mandate of the mission was to prevent avoidable ethnic conflict. The mission constantly mediated between groups and the authorities in matters like the misuse of power and the excessive use of force. This highlights a key issue: as noted above, human rights as perceived in the West never really existed in the area. Although former Yugoslavia had formal guarantees, in practice the society failed, and still fails, to provide the necessary mechanisms for all citizens to fight for redress of abuses. This was particularly evident with regard to ethnic tensions in areas like Kosovo, which would not have been so problematic in a truly democratic society. What is needed is a modern democratic independent institution such as an ombudsman. While they were present, the CSCE missions in Kosovo, Vojvodina and Sandjak tried to perform such a role with some limited success. Their expulsion in July 1993 left the minorities without even this limited form of protection. Albanian minority leaders claimed that repression intensified after the withdrawal of the CSCE mission, and that Albanians who had cooperated with the mission were victimized.

The situation will remain critical until there is protection against arbitrary rule, with neutral and effective institutions to deal with human rights complaints. This law and order problem is prevalent throughout the whole region, where sanctions appear to be aiding paramilitary organizations which thrive on racketeering and sanction-busting.

Macedonia

Macedonia retains its historical role as a Balkan trouble-spot. Tensions between the majority of Macedonians and the Albanians have continued. A referendum on autonomy for the Albanians in Macedonia was held in January 1992. More than 90 per cent of the electorate voted, with over 99

per cent voting for autonomy. Tensions rose in November 1991 over the wording of the new constitution, with the Macedonian nationalist party VMRO-DPMNE wanting a more nationalistic wording while the Albanian PDP wanted the Albanian language to have equal status with Macedonian and a formulation which would specifically include the Albanians as an integral component. More serious, perhaps, was the declaration of an autonomous republic of 'Ilirida' centred on Tetovo.

However, there have been no further developments and the PDP leader Nezrat Halili has maintained fairly good relations with President Gligorov. In mid-1992 the authorities, 16 months after the elections, finally allowed the Tetovo municipal government to take office. A worrying move occurred in January 1993 when the Macedonian members abandoned the Albanian-dominated Tetovo assembly and formed their own parallel Macedonian one. Halili has been ambivalent about the whole nature of Macedonia, and the Macedonian Albanians have always looked to Kosovo; virtually all Albanian university students from Macedonia attend Pristina University. In 1989/90, out of 71,505 pupils continuing into higher education in Macedonia, only 2,794 were Albanians. At the university level the situation was even worse. Out of 22,994 registered students in 1991/2, only 386 were ethnic Albanians, while 172 were Turks and 14 Roma. Teaching is only in Macedonian.[2] Albanians also boycotted the census (provoking endless polemics about how many Albanians actually live in the republic), the Macedonian independence referendum and the vote on the constitution.

The fall of the Macedonian government on 16 July 1992 after its failure to receive international recognition for the republic owing to Greece's veto over the name has allowed the formation of a coalition government containing five Albanians and one Turk. This is a promising development in an area where nationalist majority governments predominate (another exception to date has been Bulgaria). However the radical wing of the nationalist VMRO-DPMNE, which has displayed pro-Bulgarian sympathies, is arming itself in the mixed western parts against the Albanians, and many Albanians, especially in Tetovo, view the Albanian government members as little short of traitors to their cause. PDP delegates claimed that the Macedonians prevented them from meeting with Turkish President Ozal on 18 February 1993,[3] and the Albanian parties have petitioned international bodies to demand safeguards for ethnic Albanian rights before recognition of the republic.

In November 1993 nine ethnic Albanians including Hisen Haskaj, Assistant Deputy Minister in the coalition government, were arrested

while another ethnic Albanian government minister, the deputy health minister Imer Imeri, sought refuge in the German consulate. Skopje television, alleging cooperation between the group and Kosovo and Albania, reported that the accused were in possession of 300 machine guns and planned an armed uprising of 20,000 Albanians to create a republic of 'Ilirida' and join Albania.[4] The changes were denied both by Albania, which alleged that the whole plot was a Belgrade-inspired fabrication similar to the earlier call for an 'Ilirida',[5] and by Ibrahim Rugova in Kosovo. The initial PDP response was remarkably muted, however, merely pointing out that arms smuggling was part of a general insecurity felt by many citizens and was to some extent to be expected after the withdrawal of the JNA (the Yugoslav army), but that now a Macedonian army existed the situation had changed.[6]

The two communities are as far apart as ever. Mutual misunderstanding and distrust are widespread. The potential for conflict remains acute, as was demonstrated by allegations in mid-1993 that Albanians were trying to force 'Christian' villagers to sell their homes to ethnic Albanians in Aracino near Skopje. The distrust and antagonism of the past may yet lead to inter-ethnic conflict and even civil war, and there have been recent reports of Albanian gangs terrorizing Slav Macedonian villages in Western Macedonia. On the other hand, the Macedonian police (of whom few, if any, are ethnic Albanians) reportedly opened fire on Albanian youths in the village of Velesht near Struga in October 1993, an incident which resulted in demands by local Albanians for ethnic Albanians to constitute half of the force.[7] The economy, as elsewhere in former Yugoslavia with the partial exception of Slovenia, is in dire straits. This is exacerbated by Greek hostility to the south and the official embargo against Serbia to the north. On top of everything there remains the possibility of an explosion in Kosovo, with the likelihood of massive refugee flows which could drastically destabilize the whole situation.

Other minorities

The phenomenon of *Roma* claiming to be Egyptians, presumably to try to escape the stigma of being considered gypsies, began in Macedonia. However their situation in Macedonia is better than anywhere else in the Balkans, particularly as regards everyday racism, and they have their own media and some education outlets.

Tensions have risen over Islamicized Macedonians and *Muslim* refugees from Bosnia-Herzegovina. While the communist authorities actively encouraged smaller Muslim groups, such as the Turks and the

Muslim Macedonians, to assert their own identity, fearing that these groups were becoming Albanianized, the authorities now appear nervous of possible leverage by Turkey, the main regional power. They turned down a request by a number of Islamicized Macedonians in Debar region for schooling in Turkish rather than Macedonian. The presidium of the Republican Community of Islamicized Macedonians issued a statement in early January 1993 that the Democratic Party of Turks in Macedonia (DPTM) was behind the 'pan-Turkish ideas' in the Mosa Pijade school – the centre of the controversy, which was demolished on 28/29 December 1992.[8] The DPTM, for its part, told the CSCE mission in January 1993 that the status of the Turkish minority was under threat.[9] Construction of a refugee village in the Skopje suburb of Djorce Petrov, with financial aid from Germany, to help house the influx of Muslims fleeing Bosnia-Herzegovina was halted after protests and demonstrations by local inhabitants in February 1993.

To complicate matters the *Serbian* minority (some 44,159 or 2.2 per cent as of March 1991, although it claims up to 300,000 people) has been holding marches and protesting about its lack of recognition as a minority. Under the old Yugoslav system, the Serbs, as one of the 'nations of Yugoslavia', were of course not a minority, and it is surprising that the Macedonian authorities have been so lax in addressing the new situation of their status in the republic – especially given Serbia's position and the activity of Seselj's radicals in attempting to create a Serbian Autonomous Region of the Kumanovo Valley and the Skopska Crna Gora. The Association of Serbs and Montenegrins in Macedonia points to the problems of education in Serbian: there is, moreover, not a single radio or television programme for Serbs even though Turks, Roma and even Vlachs (who speak a form of Romanian) have both educational facilities and media outlets. Members of the association also complained that they had received no replies from the relevant authorities regarding these points. The 1993 New Year incident in the village of Kuceviste, when police clashed with Serb youths, highlighted the problems. Finally the authorities agreed to grant them the same rights and recognition as other minorities.

The church issue has further complicated matters. The Macedonian Autocephalous Orthodox Church, proclaimed in 1967 to be an integral part of the creation of a Macedonian nation, has never been recognized by the Serbian Orthodox hierarchy (nor, indeed, by other Orthodox churches). The Serbian Church, while continuing to try to bring the Macedonian Church back within its jurisdiction, has grudgingly accepted

that buildings constructed since 1967 belong to the Macedonian Church. However, it views the churches and monasteries which date from before then as its property and wants them returned.[10]

The CSCE mission

The CSCE has a mission in place in Macedonia with similar objectives to that in Kosovo. It consists of a civilian mission based in Skopje and regional monitoring centres in Tetovo and Kumanovo. Macedonia, being a part of former Yugoslavia, also comes under the remit of Geert Ahrens's working group on minorities, which has been active in trying to help the authorities resolve problems over minority groups. The Macedonian authorities, unlike those in Kosovo, have shown a willingness to undertake measures to alleviate the current situation. Outside bodies like Ahrens's working group also appear to have been relatively successful in playing an advisory and mediating role. Given the difficulties, however, any optimism must be guarded.

There is agreement on revising the constitution so that it becomes a citizen's constitution rather than one based on a dominant nation with minorities, or on two nations (i.e. including the Albanians as an integral part) and minorities, or on a federation. This proposed constitution would also make no mention of the Macedonian Orthodox Church. However, its acceptance needs a two-thirds majority in parliament, and thus support from VMRO-DPMNE. This is proving problematic.

Agreement has been reached on the under-representation of Albanians in the media, and possible funding may be made available to rectify this. On the language issue and the transcription of identity cards there has been some progress, with agreement that Albanian names can be in the original but that the forms are not bilingual. The previous regulations had stated that all school documents, however insignificant, should be in Macedonian as well as Albanian in Albanian schools. Some Albanians refused to comply and were consequently fined. Again a compromise has now been reached whereby this regulation applies only to main documents. Fines continue to be imposed but are not paid. The creation of an Albanian faculty in Skopje is under consideration, and between 40 and 50 new secondary classes with Albanian teachers have been established. There is also agreement over textbooks and measures to get more Albanians into higher education.

Both sides agree on the need to solve the vexed question of a reliable census – currently the Albanians claim 35–48 per cent of the population, while the government figure is only 21 per cent; similarly, the Serbs

claim far higher figures than official statistics. One aspect that needs addressing is the lack of representation of Albanians at all levels. Little progress is being made owing in part to the enormous economic difficulties, although recognition may help alleviate the situation. Local autonomy is also needed to combat the tendency towards centralization, a common Balkan problem. Municipalities including the Albanian-dominated Tetovo and Gostivar do at least have provisions for local self-government, even if there are problems of implementation. Agreement was also reached over the display of national symbols: the Albanian flag may be displayed at the same time as the Macedonian national flag, but not alone. This compromise is common to other countries, including Germany. Ahrens's group has also had trilateral talks with the government and Serbian minority representatives to try to solve the problems peculiar to this minority.

Albania

After decades of almost total isolation Albania finally opened itself up to the outside world. The long period of isolation, combined with acute internal economic problems, resulted in a massive wave of emigration to Italy and Greece, as well as on a smaller scale to Yugoslavia. Most fled the country via its southern border with Greece; the tensions resulting from this have combined with tensions over the position of the *Greek minority* in Albania. Although Albanian Greeks were initially received without apparent hostility by Greece, deportations back to Albania began in the second half of January 1991. Immigrants kept on coming, however, and deportations also continued. In late 1991 reports in Albania alleged that Albanians in Greece were being subjected to ill-treatment and forced to accept passports with the names changed (presumably Hellenicized).[11]

By the end of 1991 the Greek authorities appeared to have had enough of the thousands of Albanians streaming into the country with little or no means of support, and the subsequent rise in crimes. Tanjug reported on 26 December that there were over 100,000 Albanian citizens in Greece but that only a few had valid papers. Between May and December 1991 Greece had expelled 81,908 Albanians and announced that between 800 and 1,500 had been turned back at the Greek border in the preceding few weeks. The Albanian authorities protested at what they saw as discrimination and at the mass arrest of Albanians in an operation they termed 'The Broom'.[12] The Albanian Foreign Minister summoned the Greek Ambassador in Tirana on 14 January 1992 to

complain of the 'cruel treatment' of a group of Albanian citizens by Greek soldiers that had resulted in two deaths and four seriously injured people being deposited over the border near the Vidohove crossing.[13] The continuing acute economic crisis in Albania, however, means that no immediate end to the pressure to emigrate appears likely, and Albanian complaints of ill-treatment and expulsion have continued. Greek government estimates in January 1993 put the number of illegal immigrants in Greece at 434,000, of whom 185,000 (40 per cent) were Albanians.[14] A significant number of citizens of Albania have applied to change or change back their names to Greek forms, presumably hoping to be able to emigrate to or work in Greece more easily. This illustrates another important feature of the Balkans (and of countries such as Hungary, Germany and Israel) – namely that because of the 'ethnic' conception of the state, those seen as belonging to the ethnic nation who are in fact citizens of foreign states are perceived as 'fellow nationals' and often given preferential treatment in matters like immigration.

Relations between Greece and Albania have also deteriorated over the southern provinces of Albania and the Greek minority there. While Greece has consistently denied having any ethnic minorities itself, it claims 400,000 ethnic Greeks living in southern Albania. This enormous figure used to be seriously claimed only by Greek émigré sources but now appears to be repeated by official sources. The estimate is based on records of all Orthodox Christian subjects in the area, whether ethnic Albanians, Greeks, Slavs, Vlachs or Roma, and raises again the problem of the Greek tendency to confuse religion and nationality. The position of the Greek Archbishop of the Albanian Autocephalous Church is becoming increasingly problematic, and Athens has concerns over the new education bill in Albania, fearing that it will close most Greek schools in the area – a fear which is denied by Albania. In fact in Gjirokastër district there are 21 Greek elementary and 22 secondary schools, a teacher training college, and a chair of Greek language and literature at the university; there are 18 such schools in Sarande district, and 12 in Delvine district.

The deterioration in relations between the two countries began over the election in March 1992. The new election law forbade parties based on 'ethnic principles' and thus stopped Omonia, the main Greek organization, from standing. However Omonia placed their 29 candidates on the Human Rights Union list, which thenceforth was seen by all as representing the ethnic Greek vote. Albania also alleged Greek 'interference' over 'chauvinist and nationalist' pamphlets distributed 'illegally'

in Greek-inhabited areas.[15] In the event, the Human Rights Union got just 2.9 per cent of the vote and only 1.4 per cent of the assembly seats. Local elections later in the year saw its share of the poll rise to 4.3 per cent. There are also 13 Greek commune councillors, 32 councillors on municipal councils, 53 councillors on district councils, one mayor and three district chairmen, as well as press outlets. Omonia's previous policy of improvements for ethnic Greeks within Albania has been progressively abandoned in favour of either autonomy or enosis (complete unity with Greece along the line of the Shkumbi river).[16] As internal economic crisis paralysed Albania, many people in the southern areas looked towards Greece for the functions of government, and the recently opened consulates in Korce, Sarande and Gjirokastër are replacing Tirana as loci of power and authority.

Although there have been some signs of inter-ethnic cooperation, such as the joint Albanian and Greek companies in Gjirokastër, tensions are growing. Many Albanians have reacted strongly to actions by the Greek Archbishop of the Albanian Autocephalous Church, Anastasios Yanoulloutos, who was enthroned on 2 August 1992, and have demanded his withdrawal. Greece responded by threatening 'repercussions' if provisions restricting Greek minority religious rights – i.e. the Archbishop's dismissal – were passed by the Albanian parliament; it appealed to both the CSCE and the Council of Europe. However, the Albanians reacted against what they perceived as Greek interference in the draft law on church–state relations in Albania. Matters came to a head in June 1993 with the deportation of the Greek Orthodox Archimandrite Khristostonmos Maidhonis for 'openly irredentist activity',[17] which was followed by mass expulsions of Albanians from Greece in retaliation. Meanwhile in Greece pressure is growing and the Albanians appear increasingly impotent in the face of incidents such as occurred when the ethnic Greek Olympic athlete Piro Dhima was fêted in Greece, in the name of the Greek Prime Minister, as a Greek from 'non-liberated lands'.[18]

Developments in *other minority groups*, besides Macedonian and Serb/Montenegrin organizations, include the Wallachians Association (for Vlachs) whose chair Jorgo Balamacin met President Berisha on 12 February 1993.

Greece

The position of minorities in Greece itself – whether they be Turks, Vlachs, Slav Macedonians, Pomaks, Albanians or Roma – remains as awkward as ever and has become exacerbated by the name issue between Greece and Macedonia and the rise in Greek nationalism, so much so that discussion of the minority situation is problematic even for ethnic Greeks.

The Greek government's extreme sensitivity over the name issue has been demonstrated by a series of arrests and trials of left-wing Greeks for attempting to criticize its refusal to move on the question of recognition for Macedonia. Six members of a group called 'The Organization for the Reconstruction of the KKE' (OAKKE) were tried on 27 January 1992 and sentenced to six and a half months' imprisonment for fly-posting demands to 'Recognize Independent Slav Macedonia'. Four students, members of a 'Coalition Against Nationalism and War', were sentenced to 19 months' imprisonment for distributing a leaflet entitled 'The neighbouring peoples are not our enemies'. In both cases the accused were released pending appeal. The hearings will not take place until 1995 – a hopeful sign, which may indicate that the courts are reluctant to be so obviously used by the executive. Five other left-wing Greeks tried for the publication and distribution of a pamphlet on Macedonia were acquitted. Two Macedonian activists were each sentenced to five months' imprisonment and large fines on 1 April 1993 for similarly exercising their right to freedom of expression regarding the Macedonian issue. It was reported that the Orthodox Greek hierarchy initially relieved Archimandrite Nikodimos Tsarknias of his duties in his parish outside Thessalonika because he had identified himself as a Macedonian, and that it then expelled him from the church.[19]

There has, however, been a slight relaxation as regards the situation of *ethnic Turks* in Greece. The 100,000 or so Turks of Western Thrace have for some time been under considerable pressure from the authorities and have complained of severely curtailed educational facilities in Turkish language schools, the imposition by the authorities of their official candidates as muftis and on community boards despite the adverse wishes of the minority population, and official obstruction in granting building permits to ethnic Turks. Nevertheless, ethnic Turks are now able to buy and sell land and repair mosques, although serious problems relating to education, expropriation of land, and the choosing of muftis and pious foundations remain.

On the other hand, the Greek government remains obdurate over

Macedonia but is officially committed to the current Greek/Albanian border. Public opinion inside Greece, combined with further collapse within Albania, may force the issue. Either way, Greece's rejection of any concept of minorities within its own borders, while claiming those in Albania as Greek, remains as strong as ever and appears to be gaining in public support. Internally the traditional Greek confusion of citizenship, nationality and religion remains.

Bulgaria

In contrast to much of the Balkans, post-Zhivkov Bulgaria has, in the main, remained a beacon of hope in the field of inter-ethnic relations, with the exception of the Roma. In the October 1991 elections the *ethnic Turkish* party, the Movement for Rights and Freedoms (DPS) gained 24 members of parliament, over 650 village mayors, 1,000 councillors and 20 municipal mayors, and held the balance of power between the former communists and the Union of Democratic Forces (UDF). Despite the constitutional ban on solely ethnic-based parties, the Constitutional Court narrowly ruled that the DPS was legal.[20] It did not formally enter government but instead embarked on a *de facto* coalition whereby it shared the parliamentary commissions with the UDF, which kept the ex-communists firmly out in the cold. The DPS called off school boycotts after the government introduced four Turkish language classes a week for ethnic Turks.

This unofficial coalition broke down, however, over the economic policies of Filip Dimitrov's government, which were causing a new mass exodus of ethnic Turks in the southern region around Kardzhali. The price of tobacco, a staple crop in the south, fell by half and unemployment soared to 40 per cent for ethnic Turks in July 1993, with some settlements experiencing 80 per cent.[21] In addition, the government's policies on land privatization meant that the ethnic Turks who until then had worked the land would be unable to become owners. Rumours of a new census in Turkey and of regulations that all those in Turkey at that time would be registered as Turkish citizens also played a part. President Zhelev confirmed in August 1993 that some 80,000 ethnic Turks had recently left and another 140,000 had applied for emigration to Turkey for economic reasons.[22] The DPS, faced with the severe erosion of its electoral base, began to distance itself from the government and called for Dimitrov's removal. At the same time Turkey announced tougher immigration measures in October to try to stem the flood. It seems that

the ethnic Turks are experiencing a shift from country to town similar to that of the Slav Bulgarians in the 1950s and 1960s. Now, however, with the greater international freedom of movement, they are choosing to move to Turkish rather than to Bulgarian cities. The education programme for ethnic Turks remains woefully inadequate and this tendency towards emigration looks likely to continue. (It must also be noted that, in common with other former communist Balkan states, there is a massive outflow of the young intelligentsia of the majority populations, to such an extent that some see this as a veritable demographic disaster.)

The ensuing stalemate in the formation of a government was eventually broken when a 'cabinet of experts' was set up under the DPS mandate. It was led by Professor Lyuben Berov, with the non-Turkish DPS member Evgeni Matinchev as a Deputy Prime Minister and also Minister for Labour and Social Welfare. It would appear that the intelligent non-confrontational approach taken by the leadership of the DPS has played a constructive role in making Bulgaria something of an exception in Balkan nationalist politics. The DPS still retains the bulk of the ethnic Turkish vote, despite the appearance of a more radical and so far officially unrecognized rival ethnic-Turkish party – the Turkish Democratic Party – headed by expelled DPS member Adem Kenan, as well as the Muslim Party of Justice, led by the former and somewhat discredited Chief Mufti Nedim Genzhev.

The enforced isolation of the *Pomaks* (Islamicized Slavs), inhabiting inaccessible closed border regions between Bulgaria and Greece, has to some extent been lifted. In Bulgaria there is a marked tendency for polarization between those who move to the towns and, by losing their religious identity, become associated with the Bulgarian majority, and those who are becoming Turkified with the help of a shared religion. There is, indeed, a radical element among the DPS calling for Turkish education among the Pomaks for this very purpose.[23] The Democratic Party of Labour, headed by Kamen Burov, was set up in December 1992 to defend Pomak interests, and is very close to the DPS. It appears that this minority is gradually dividing itself between self-styled Bulgarians and Turks, and may eventually disappear.

The smaller Greek-speaking *Sarakatsani* group, on the other hand, may well find that the end of the Cold War and the ensuing demilitarization of the Rhodope border will allow them to renew contacts in Greece and thus preserve and strengthen their national identity. There is also an Association of *Vlachs* based in Vidin which protested at not being listed in the December 1992 census.[24]

The situation of the *Roma* remains problematic, as it has done throughout the Balkans. The fledgling Roma parties, despite becoming more assertive, remain fragmented and divided along religious and occupational and traditional settler/nomadic lines. They suffer from the constitutional ban on ethnic and religious parties which the DPS managed to circumvent. A rising crime rate in which the Roma were seen as the culprits – official statistics for 1992 state that they comprised a third of the over 70,000 criminals apprehended[25] – bolstered the public perception of the Roma and led to a rise in social tensions. Serious clashes with the police broke out in Plovdiv, Haskovo and Pazardzhik – the most serious in Plovdiv in August 1992, when a bystander was killed and many were wounded. The minority suffers from institutionalized racism as well as from acute economic problems: in some areas almost all Roma are unemployed. This problem was acknowledged when President Zhelev met representatives of the United Romany Organization led by Vasil Chaprazov in November 1992 and announced that his advisers would draw up a short-term programme on employment for Roma.[26]

Problems also remain over those in Pirin Macedonia in the southwest who espouse a separate *Macedonian* identity. The main organization for such people is the UMO-Ilinden (United Macedonian Organization), founded soon after Zhivkov's fall but continually denied registration and subject to various forms of official harassment in the recent past.[27] For the first time since 1965, the December 1992 census allowed such people to state that they were Macedonian, and UMO-Ilinden was active in distributing leaflets prior to the census in Pirin region which caused a Bulgarian nationalist backlash. The census results on ethnic breakdown are not yet available.

Conclusion

Until the societies of this region develop their own adequate institutions, there is a need for CSCE and similar missions in acute trouble-spots like Kosovo and Macedonia, as well as for 'transnational regimes' and support from the international community for the whole area. However, the danger of overstretching UN and other resources should always be borne in mind. The capability of the international community to pacify such deep-rooted conflicts as are found in the Balkans may be limited. For example, in the past five years the UN has been involved in more peacekeeping operations than in all the previous 43 years put together. Conflict resolution mechanisms need immeasurable strengthening in key

bodies like the CSCE. With the end of the bloc mentality, a shift is needed from the previous emphasis on military bodies like NATO to those promoting peaceful development. However, while a steady movement towards a truly democratic society is perhaps the only guarantee that minority and other rights will be respected, for the immediate future – as long as the fighting continues in the former Yugoslavia the war psychosis will also continue and will adversely affect the Kosovo problem. In the short term perhaps the most that can be hoped for is that all parties in Kosovo and Macedonia see it as in their interests not to start major hostilities there.

The history of minority treatment and the international response to flagrant violations of rights do not allow one to be particularly sanguine. The current situation in Serbia may indicate that punitive measures like sanctions have the unforeseen side-effect of aiding sections within society, such as paramilitaries, who are part of the problem in developing internal democratic institutions. This is quite apart from the question of whether sanctions have the desired effect of forcing change on recalcitrant nationalist leaders (it can be argued that they actually helped Milosevic and Seselj in the December 1992 elections). Balkan nationalism as shown by Serbia and Greece and others is particularly volatile and outside pressure runs the risk of exacerbating it. Internal mediation appears to be a better method than threats.

On the other hand, the West does have the positive tools of aid and support and perhaps these could be used to better effect to back up minority rights. Efforts such as Macedonia's should be supported, not ignored. To abandon Macedonia on account of Greece's veto merely increases the chance of social breakdown and civil war there. In a similar vein the restraint of the Kosovo Albanians in the face of acute repression at the very least deserves commendation.

Notes

The source of much of the material cited here is the BBC's Summary of World Broadcasts, Eastern Europe (SWB EE). See also *East European Newsletter*, vol. 6, no. 11, 25 May 1992; *Turkey Briefing*, vol. 5, no. 5, October 1991; the Helsinki Watch report on ethnic Turks in Greece, 20 April 1992, USA.

1 Tanjug, 23 November 1992, in SWB EE/1547 C1/8, 25 November 1992.
2 Aleksandar Soljakovski, 'An Education in Ethnic Complexity', *Balkan War Report*, No. 15, October 1992, London.
3 Albanian Telegraph Agency (ATA), 21 February 1993, in SWB EE/1620 C1/13, 23 February 1993.

4   Tanjug, 9 November 1993, in SWB EE/1843 C/8, 11 November 1993.
5   ATA, 12 November 1993, in SWB EE/1846 B/2, 15 November 1993.
6   Tanjug, 12 November 1993, in SWB EE/1846 C/18, 15 November 1993.
7   ATA, 22 October 1993, in SWB EE/1829, C/11, 26 October 1993.
8   Tanjug, 4 January 1993, in SWB EE/1580 C1/11, 7 January 1993.
9   Tanjug, 22 January 1993, in SWB EE/1597 C1/15, 27 January 1993.
10 For polemics and attempts to bring the Macedonian Church back under the
    control of the Serbian Church see statement by Metropolitan Jovan of
    Zagreb and Ljubljana etc. in Tanjug, 17 December 1992, in SWB EE/1570
    C1/7, 22 December 1992.
11 ATA, 14 November 1991, in SWB EE/1233 B/3, 19 November 1991.
12 SWB EE/1266 A1/1, 31 December 1991.
13 Albanian Radio, Tirana, 14 January 1992, in SWB EE/1280 ii and A1/1,
    17 January 1992.
14 Greek Radio, Athens, 29 January 1992, in SWB EE/1601 A1/3, 1 Febru-
    ary 1993.
15 Albanian Radio, Tirana, 10 March 1992, in SWB EE/1328 A1/1, 13
    March 1992.
16 James Pettifer, 'Greece: into the Balkan Crisis', *The World Today*, No-
    vember 1992.
17 ATA, 29 June 1993.
18 ATA, 13 August 1992, in SWB EE/1465 B/1, 21 August 1992.
19 See the Macedonian Information Centre, 26 October 1992.
20 Bulgarian Telegraph Agency (BTA), 21 April 1992, in SWB EE/1364 B/1,
    25 April 1992. The DPS is officially open to all groups but remains a
    predominantly ethnic Turkish party. The vote split six for and six against;
    as a simple majority is needed the ruling went in the DPS's favour.
21 BTA, 30 July 1992, in SWB EE/1451 B/6, 5 August 1992.
22 BTA, 1 August 1992, in SWB EE/1451 B/6, 5 August 1992.
23 BTA, 14 December 1992, in SWB EE/1565 B/2, 16 December 1992. In
    one case reported of school children and parents asked to complete forms
    stating ethnicity before 10 October 1992, some 2,729 (23 per cent of all
    schoolchildren in the area) had claimed to be Turkish whereas in 1991
    none had. In another case 1,174 out of a total of 1,721 identified them-
    selves as Turks. Duna, Sofia, 23, 27 and 28 November 1992, and Trud,
    Sofia, 15 December 1992, quoted in Rada Nikolaev, 'Bulgaria's 1992
    Census: Results, Problems, and Implications', *RFE/RL Research Report*,
    Vol. 2, No. 6, 5 February 1993.
24 Nikolaev, op. cit. The 1934 census gave 16,405 Vlachs while the 1956
    census only gave some 4,000.
25 BTA, 20 January 1993, in SWB EE/1594 B/1, 23 January 1993.
26 BTA, 21 November 1992, in SWB EE/1546 B/8, 24 November 1992.
27 Hugh Poulton, *The Balkans: Minorities and States in Conflict* (London:
    Minority Rights Group, 1991).

8

THE ROLE OF THE COUNCIL OF EUROPE

KLAUS SCHUMANN

After the Second World War the creation of the Council of Europe was the first political and institutional reply to the urgent need to overcome divisions and conflicts in Europe. The organization's statutory mission was to achieve a greater unity between its member countries, not only on the basis of a wide network of practical cooperation measures but, above all, on the basis of a specific political project: the commitment of member countries and their peoples to the principles of a pluralist democracy, human rights and the rule of law. This transnational concept of peaceful coexistence under a guaranteed regime of common values aimed in particular at gaining respect for the dignity of all human beings regardless of their racial, religious and other differences, and at sustained efforts towards reconciliation between peoples.

This project deliberately took into account the most striking characteristic of Europe as a continent: its diversity of peoples determined to maintain their own traditions and culture and at the same time its common experience of state-building on a territorial basis. There exist in Europe many different types of state: those made up of a population with identical traditions and cultures; multinational states within which the composite elements were given a large degree of autonomy, for instance on the federal model; and, in many cases, states made up of groups of various national, cultural or religious origins.

These situations inevitably lead to certain tensions and to differences in the search for adequate guarantees of everybody's rights. There are two main attempts at a solution:

(a) the model of society based on the universality and equality of

rights for all its members, the enjoyment of these rights being the responsibility of the state;

(b)   the attempt to establish one's identity through belonging to a community with its own specific culture, religion, ethnic origin and way of life – that is, the right to be oneself.

Both these approaches are legitimate and need democratically agreed solutions.

A society without conflict has always been a fiction of various shades of totalitarian doctrines and regimes. At present we are again living through a terrible example of such a fiction on the territory of the former Yugoslavia. The perpetrators of the ideology of 'ethnic cleansing' are pursuing a totalitarian policy not only by changing arbitrary borders on the basis of ethnic criteria, but by committing ethnically motivated acts of murder.

This situation also illustrates how closely human rights are linked to the minorities issue. It is perfectly clear that the notion that the continued existence of a state might be possible only if its population is ethnically, culturally and religiously homogeneous is in itself a violation of human rights. The basic legal definition of human rights necessarily includes a multicultural, multi-ethnic and multi-denominational vision of what constitutes a state. This also applies to regions and to the individual constituent states in a federal state.

In developing its basic concept of promoting reconciliation, mutual understanding and increased cooperation by respecting the diversity of peoples and their traditions, the Council of Europe has, over the past 45 years, contributed considerably to improving the situation of minorities within its member countries. Its aims include:

(a)   the observance of human rights for all without discrimination on any ground such as race, colour, religion, national or social origin, or association with a national minority;

(b)   the development of the scope for freedom of action in civil society, allowing groups of people to shape their own cultural, social and religious destiny;

(c)   increasing opportunities for transfrontier and regional cooperation, thus reducing the divisive effects of frontiers.

The structure of the organization has facilitated the successful combination of these different but complementary approaches. Its two statutory

organs are the Committee of Ministers, responsible for intergovernmental cooperation, including standard-setting activities in the field of human rights protection; and the Parliamentary Assembly, in which the representatives of national parliaments are associated with the development of European cooperation. The activities of the Council of Europe are, moreover, associated with those of representatives of local and regional authorities in the member countries as well as of international non-governmental organizations (NGOs). This structure has established a climate of genuine partnership, which is one characteristic of an open society.

Until 1989 a similar process was not possible in the closed societies of central and eastern Europe. The difficulties stemming from this fact are all the more serious in that, for various historical reasons, peoples of many different origins and cultures lived together in a more complex pattern in this part of Europe than anywhere else. Furthermore, the newly achieved freedom brought into the open frustrations and dissensions which for a long time had been artificially stifled by ideological constraints.

Today the Council of Europe is gradually opening up its structures and activities to all these new democracies in central and eastern Europe; some have already become full members. At the same time the organization is faced with a question that is now more acute than ever: what contribution towards solving minority issues is being or could be made by its fund of standard-setting instruments and its experience in other contexts in strengthening confidence between members of distinct groups?

The legal protection of minorities
In the standard-setting field the Council of Europe's main contribution to the protection of minorities still lies with the achievements of the European Convention on Human Rights.

The European Convention on Human Rights
The member states of the Council of Europe, all being Contracting Parties or signatories to the European Convention on Human Rights, recognize a number of fundamental human rights. This Convention is important in several respects for the protection of minorities.

First of all, the human rights recognized by the Convention are guaranteed to all persons coming under the jurisdiction of one of the

contracting states. The Convention therefore protects not only the nationals and citizens of a state, but also any other persons affected by a measure taken by the authorities of that state.

Several of the rights thus secured are of obvious interest for the protection of minorities:

(a) the right of everyone to freedom of thought, conscience and religion, including the freedom to manifest one's religion or belief, either alone or in community with others, in public or private, in worship, teaching, practice and observance (Article 9);

(b) the right of everyone to freedom of expression, including freedom to hold opinions and to receive and impart information and ideas without interference by public authorities and regardless of frontiers (Article 10);

(c) the right of everyone to freedom of peaceful assembly and to freedom of association with others (Article 11);

(d) the right to education, including the right of parents to ensure such education and teaching in conformity with their own religious and philosophical convictions (Additional Protocol, Article 2).

Moreover, the enjoyment of rights and freedoms set forth in the Convention must be secured without discrimination on any ground such as sex, race, colour, language, religion, political or other opinion, national or social origin, association with a national minority, property, birth or other status (Article 14).

It should be pointed out that some of these rights entail for those enjoying them the possibility of exercising them in community with others, that is to say collectively. This may be relevant to the situations of ethnic, national or religious minorities, particularly in the case of freedom of religion and freedom of peaceful assembly and association with others. The enjoyment of these rights must therefore also be guaranteed when their holders exercise them in a community.

Lastly, the importance of the Convention lies not only in the scope of the rights protected, but also in the machinery of protection established in Strasbourg to investigate alleged violations and to ensure respect for the obligations under the Convention. This protective machinery can function in two ways. Under the first, any State Party may apply to the European Commission of Human Rights if it considers that another State Party is not fulfilling its commitments. Under the second method, any person, NGO or other group of individuals claiming to be the victim of a

violation of the rights set forth in the Convention may apply directly to the European Commission of Human Rights. In the case of each application which is declared admissible by the Commission, the quasi-judicial – or, when it comes to the European Court of Human Rights, even fully judicial – proceedings will result in a binding decision. This will be in the form of either a judgment by the Court or a decision by the Committee of Ministers of the Council of Europe, which, in addition, supervises the enforcement of these decisions by the states concerned. By means of this system, the European Convention on Human Rights has established a collective guarantee, at Council of Europe level, for the respect of human rights.

Further steps towards the protection of the rights of minorities
The European Convention on Human Rights has proved to be a dynamic instrument. The European Commission and Court of Human Rights, as the supervisory organs, through their increasingly extensive body of case law, have developed the scope of the obligations under the Convention to suit the evolving situation. Furthermore, the member states themselves have on several occasions supplemented the list of rights set forth in the Convention by means of additional protocols.

However, European developments since 1989 have shown that the protection of national minorities has become a matter of extreme urgency. The Parliamentary Assembly of the Council of Europe feels that the definition and effective guarantee of the rights of national minorities are an unavoidable obligation of the international community. Effective legal protection of minorities' rights is considered to be one of the paths that must be followed in order to try to defuse ethnic conflicts and lay lasting foundations for peace on the European continent.

Within this context, the European Commission for Democracy through Law, known as the Venice Commission – a body of eminent constitutional experts set up in 1989, as a partial agreement, under the aegis of the Council of Europe – took the initiative in working out the proposal for a draft European Convention for the Protection of Minorities. This proposal has been submitted for consideration to the Committee of Ministers, the organization's decision-making body.

The Parliamentary Assembly, for its part, chose not to prepare a new specific legal instrument to protect the rights of minorities, with all the risks inherent in having several judicial bodies with responsibility for human rights. It preferred instead to use the existing system by adopting at the beginning of February 1993 the text of the proposal for an

Additional Protocol to the Convention for the Protection of Human Rights and Fundamental Freedoms, concerning National Minorities and their Members. Such a protocol would fall under the authority and competence of the universally recognized machinery of the Convention. This would enable persons belonging to minorities to benefit from the only protection system of its kind in the world, the direct individual or collective petition to the European Commission and subsequently to the European Court of Human Rights. By recommending this protocol to the Convention, the Parliamentary Assembly wanted to guarantee not just non-discrimination by the Convention, but also positive rights for persons belonging to national minorities.

The Assembly's recommendation for an additional protocol to the Human Rights Convention, as well as the Venice Commission's proposal for a separate Convention on the protection of minorities, have been forwarded for consideration by the Committee of Ministers to an intergovernmental Committee of Experts. This committee is to propose specific legal standards relating to the protection of national minorities, taking into account the work carried out within the United Nations, and also the activities of the Council of Europe and CSCE. At the first meeting of heads of member states, held in October 1993 in Vienna, the Council of Europe agreed to call for a new 'framework convention specifying the principles which contracting states commit themselves to respect, in order to assure the protection of national minorities. This instrument would also be open for signature by non-member states.' They also agreed to begin work on drafting 'a protocol complementing the European Convention on Human Rights in the cultural field by provisions guaranteeing individual rights, in particular for persons belonging to national minorities'. The same meeting agreed to overhaul and speed up the procedure for hearing complaints by establishing a single European Court of Human Rights to supersede the present system of two bodies (the European Commission of Human Rights and the European Court of Human Rights).[1]

The protection of regional or minority languages

The idea of a Charter on European Regional or Minority Languages was first proposed by the Standing Conference of Local and Regional Authorities of Europe, which drew up the draft for such a Charter. The initiative received the full support of the Parliamentary Assembly. The Committee of Ministers subsequently instructed an intergovernmental Committee of Experts to prepare a draft text. In June 1992, the Commit-

tee of Ministers adopted, as a Convention, the European Charter for Regional or Minority Languages. This aims to ensure, as far as possible, the use of regional or minority languages in education and the media, and to permit their use in judicial and administrative settings, economic and social life, and cultural activities. The Charter, on which legislation in Council of Europe member states should be based, will also be able to give guidance to many other states on a difficult and sensitive subject because it can benefit minorities whose most distinctive feature is, in fact, their language.

Ad hoc mechanisms for the protection of human rights
Against the background of the massive and flagrant violations of human rights in the territory of former Yugoslavia, Lord Owen, the co-Chairman of the International Conference on Peace in Former Yugoslavia, proposed in his address to the Parliamentary Assembly on 3 October 1992 that the Council of Europe should provide European non-member states with an ad hoc mechanism for the protection of human rights.

This proposal was carefully examined by the Committee of Ministers, which agreed in principle to make arrangements whereby the Council of Europe helps European states which are not yet members of the Council of Europe. It would contribute, as a transitional measure, to the establishment, within the internal legal system of these states, of a body responsible for ensuring observance of respect for human rights that would take into account the substantive provisions of the European Convention on Human Rights. The establishment of such a transitional human rights control mechanism, drawing on the competence and the experience of the control organs of the European Convention, might also promote the process of accession to the Council of Europe. The Committee of Ministers subsequently informed the Geneva Conference that the Council of Europe was ready to contribute to ensuring respect for human rights in European non-member states and, as soon as there was a request from such a state, to appoint specially qualified persons to sit on a court or other internal body legally responsible for ensuring respect for human rights. The first practical implementation of such an ad hoc mechanism for the protection of human rights could take place (hopefully soon) in the context of negotiations for a new constitution for Bosnia-Herzegovina within the framework of the Geneva Conference. One of the first items to be taken up in such negotiations will be the regulation of human rights. It is, therefore, very important that the Conference can already rely on the Council of Europe's contribution to the establishment

of an ad hoc mechanism; it is also possible that a Human Rights Court may be set up as part of the interim arrangements under which Bosnia-Herzegovina will be governed while the constitution is being negotiated.

Confidence-building measures and pilot projects to assist minorities

Apart from its contribution to the legal protection of individual freedom in general and minority rights in particular, the Council of Europe, through its transnational concept of peaceful coexistence, has striven ever since its foundation to foster the internal stability of member countries by promoting mutual understanding and strengthening confidence in human relations.

Confidence-building as part of the programme of activities

Many of the Council of Europe's daily activities include considerable achievements in this confidence-building field – primarily in dealing with the diversity of life in multicultural societies, including the response to the appearance of pockets of deprivation and social exclusion. Cooperation focuses on the following priorities:

(a) in the educational and cultural field, devising intercultural teaching methods based on respect for individual dignity and spiritual values, and on the rights of minority groups, allowing them to express themselves freely;

(b) in the social field, promoting community relations between immigrant groups and the host country, based on mutual understanding, respect for diversity and the involvement of all in social progress;

(c) in the institutional field, promoting local self-government, partly through legal instruments such as the Charter of Local Self-government;

(d) in the political and legal field, formulating fundamental principles common to every democratic and pluralist society, such as the 'Declaration on Intolerance – a Threat to Democracy', adopted by the Committee of Ministers on 17 May 1981.

The Council of Europe's working methods are flexible and easily adaptable to new needs. Its achievements are not restricted to member states; for example, through its ever-increasing programme of cooperation with and assistance for countries of central and eastern Europe, the organization is also gradually opening its intergovernmental structures to all these

new democracies for their participation as observers. Ten of these countries are already Parties to the European Cultural Convention and therefore participate as full members in all activities related to culture, education, architectural heritage, sport and youth. All the above-mentioned findings can be applied in practice in multicultural societies specifically faced with the issue of national minorities.

Practical on-the-spot measures through pilot projects

Any steps to establish a climate of confidence must primarily be taken on the spot through measures specifically designed to promote relations between minorities and the majority in given situations.

One method already used by the Council of Europe – in the field of multicultural education and community relations – has been to conduct pilot projects in sites chosen for their practical interest with regard to minority problems. In the context of its contacts and cooperation with countries of central and eastern Europe, the Council of Europe is developing similar pragmatic pilot projects with the following aims:

(a) to promote mutual acquaintance and understanding with a view to peaceful coexistence;
(b) to combat racism, intolerance and xenophobia through the application of non-violent solutions;
(c) to break down barriers between different communities through schemes based on a shared experience, encompassing human rights and peace studies, and intercultural activities.

The initiators of the pilot projects may be member or non-member countries, regions or local authorities, schools or universities, NGOs or the media. The fields covered by such projects are mainly education, culture, media, youth, legal, political and social questions, local democracy and the environment.

The examples below give an idea of the range of possible projects and the variety of approaches, although this does not mean that agreement has already been reached among potential partners.

Amongst the conclusions and recommendations presented by Mr Mazowiecki, the Special Rapporteur of the United Nations Commission on Human Rights on the situation of human rights in the territory of the former Yugoslavia, the necessity for democratic and tolerant *media* is strongly underlined:

In most parts of the former Yugoslavia, there is a need for support and assistance to be provided to democratically oriented groups. The information blockade which prevails in the region should be broken. Support should be given to initiatives taken by independent groups, both within and outside the former Yugoslavia, which aim to provide objective information.

Indeed, the Council of Europe considers a typical pilot project to be support for independent radio stations open to all nationalities and cultures present in the region and broadcasting bi- or multilingual programmes – that is, using the tremendous appeal of a medium such as radio with the positive aim of building up confidence among the various communities living in the region. This dissemination of an increased body of objective information, greater knowledge and free expression of different cultures, including those of minorities, is regarded as an effective means of defusing political conflicts. Indeed, the Council of Europe is already supporting the project of an independent Radio Rijeka-Fiume International, whose programmes are intended for all linguistic communities living in Istria.

Education is another important source of the bias and prejudices which play a significant part in determining perceptions of other people. The teaching of history is, therefore, another priority project among confidence-building measures, and indeed has always been a priority activity in the Council of Europe's educational programmes, since it is so important in shaping young people's attitudes towards other countries, races and religions. The discovery of 'others' must be the discovery of a relationship and not of a barrier. The aims and content of such a pilot project in a given geographical area (for example, Austria, Hungary, Slovenia, Slovakia and Romania) would be to study prejudices in the teaching of the history of the countries concerned, with a view to dispelling them; to work out a tolerant, impartial approach to history and hence to strengthen mutual confidence. As a working method, a team of experts on history teaching from the countries concerned could be set up, 'assisted' by experts from the Council of Europe who have undertaken similar experiments in the past.

This example of a pilot project aims at bringing together partners in the context of transfrontier cooperation. Long-term regional and cross-border cooperation is essential for strengthening mutual confidence, reducing tensions and stabilizing a region. Over the past few decades, the Council of Europe and its Standing Conference of Local and

Regional Authorities of Europe have given their strong support to the development of such *Euroregions* (e.g. Regio Basiliensis, Arge Alpe-Adria), and will actively continue to do so for projects of this kind in central and eastern Europe. An excellent recent example was the launching of the new Carpathian Euroregion. The fact that such a project could be set up in a sensitive area, including Poland, Ukraine, Slovakia, Hungary, and hopefully soon Romania, proves that countries that have freed themselves from totalitarian regimes are capable of genuine cooperation in rediscovering elements of their historical relationship. The project aims to expand bilateral ties and to develop collaboration in education, health care, environmental protection, and cultural and scientific fields. The Council of Europe considers this initiative to be a typical pilot project and is providing active support for the implementation of the various cooperation programmes. In January 1993, Russia and the Nordic countries agreed to revive the thousand-year-old ties between east and west across Europe's Arctic tip, which had been broken for decades by the Cold War, by setting up the so-called Barents Euro-Arctic Council. Many similar initiatives exist elsewhere for regional cooperation across borders which have previously formed ideological barriers.

Conclusion

The Council of Europe's activities in the standard-setting field, together with its whole activity as a multilateral cooperation network at governmental, parliamentary, regional and local levels, undertaken in close collaboration with NGOs, are directed at fostering mutual understanding and reinforcing confidence in human relations. Today the organization – which operates on a pan-European level and is open to all countries of the European continent – contributes to legal and democratic security, to domestic stability and to the improvement of relations between countries and peoples in the humanitarian, social and cultural fields. For the countries of central and eastern Europe, which still suffer considerable identity problems, this concept of European cooperation, in preparation for future European integration, is becoming increasingly attractive. It is seen as a vital alternative to the concept of the all-sovereign nation-state which is being presented again by those who want to maintain or acquire political power by undemocratic means, as the ultimate justification for political self-determination. For the sake of pluralist democracy, individual freedom and the respect for minority rights in Europe, therefore, it

seems essential to maintain and to strengthen the scope for a transnational regime through the Council of Europe and its activities.

Notes

1 'Vienna Declaration of the Council of Europe', 9 October 1993, *Europe Documents*, No. 1855, 15 October 1993.

9

THE ROLE OF THE CSCE

RICHARD DALTON*

Introduction

The CSCE has developed pragmatically, in response to changing conditions in Europe. It fills a gap in the activities of European and transatlantic institutions by being able to act collectively, through diplomacy, with reference to its set of high standards on security relations and human rights. This chapter assesses its strengths and weaknesses in dealing with problems affecting minorities and tries to answer the question: will the CSCE make a difference?

Standard-setting

All CSCE work on minorities stems from the 1975 Helsinki Final Act. Principle VII of the Declaration on Principles Guiding Relations between Participating States lays down that:

> The participating states on whose territory national minorities exist will respect the right of persons belonging to such minorities to equality before the law, will afford them the full opportunity for the actual enjoyment of human rights and fundamental freedoms and will, in this manner, protect their legitimate interests in this sphere.

This cautious, compromise language covers the position of those states which maintain that they have no minorities (especially France and Greece), emphasizes that rights are to be enjoyed and protected individu-

---

* The views expressed in this paper are the personal views of the author: they do not necessarily reflect those of the British government.

ally (hence the 'persons belonging' formula), and offered less to minorities than the United Nations Covenant on Civil and Political Rights, which lays down the right of persons belonging to minorities to enjoy their culture, to practise their religion and to use their language. The champion of the entry of minorities into the Helsinki process in those days was Yugoslavia. Most states preferred not to deal with the subject as a separate matter.

The first major change in this trend took place at the Vienna follow-up meeting, which began in 1986. The concluding document, adopted in January 1989, promised sustained efforts to implement the provisions of the Helsinki Final Act in respect of minorities. States 'will refrain from any discrimination against such persons and will contribute to the realisation of their legitimate interests and aspirations in the field of human rights and fundamental freedoms'. States will also 'protect and create conditions for the promotion of the ethnic, cultural, linguistic and religious identity of national minorities on their territory'. These commitments introduced to the CSCE the idea of positive action to assist minorities in the four areas generally recognized as indicating the existence of a separate group.

That was as far as the process went before the fall of communism. The leap forward took place at the Human Dimension Conferences in Copenhagen in 1990 and Moscow in 1991. The principles enunciated there were elaborated at a meeting of experts on minorities in Geneva in July 1991, and were added to in certain respects at the Paris summit in November 1990 and at the Helsinki follow-up meeting in 1992.

The result is a set of standards, comprising both rights and questions of public and international policy, which can be summarized as follows:[1]

(1) National minorities make a rich contribution to the life of society.
(2) Friendly relations among peoples, peace, justice, stability and democracy require that the ethnic, cultural, religious and linguistic identity of national minorities be protected and conditions for the promotion of that identity be created.
(3) To belong to a national minority is a matter for a person's individual choice and no disadvantage may arise from the exercise of such choice.[2]
(4) Rights of persons belonging to minorities are an inseparable element of universally recognized human rights. They are to be enjoyed individually as well as in community with other members of their group. Special measures are to be adopted,

where necessary, to ensure full equality with other citizens in the exercise of human rights or fundamental freedoms, such measures to take into account historical and territorial circumstances of minorities.

(5) There should be no compulsory assimilation.

(6) There should be free use of the mother tongue, with adequate opportunities for instruction of or in the mother tongue. There should be use of minority languages before public authorities wherever possible and in conformity with applicable national legislation.

(7) There should be a democratic political framework based on the rule of law, with a functioning independent judiciary; this should ensure equal rights, freedom of expression, political pluralism, social tolerance and legal rules to restrain the abuse of governmental power.

(8) There should be democratic participation in decision-making or consultative bodies, with emphasis on the importance of negotiations and consultations in solving problems.

(9) There should be equal protection for representatives of majority populations in minority areas.

(10) Observers should be present at elections held below the national level.

(11) States should create conditions for effective involvement of minorities in public life and economic activities.

(12) There should be encouragement to select constitutional devices to promote involvement of minorities in public life. At the Geneva meeting in 1991, it was agreed that: 'Aware of the diversity and varying constitutional systems among them, which make no single approach necessarily generally applicable... States note ... that positive results have been obtained by some of them in an appropriate democratic manner by' [there follows a list of constitutional devices ranging from advisory bodies through decentralized government to the encouragement of grass-roots community relations efforts – full text in Annex I].

(13) There should be effective measures to prevent discrimination against individuals, particularly in employment, housing and education, including a broad array of administrative and judicial remedies.

(14) Persons belonging to minorities should have the same rights and the same duties of citizenship as the rest of the population.

(15) There should be tolerance and respect for different cultures.

(16) States should respect the right of minorities to establish and maintain organizations and associations and will encourage and not hinder the work of such organizations, groups and individuals active in fostering cross-cultural understanding.

(17) In conformity with their constitutional law, states will adopt laws prohibiting acts that constitute incitement to violence based on racial or religious discrimination or hostility, including anti-semitism, and policies to enforce such laws.

(18) The publication of data about crimes based on prejudice as to race, ethnic identity or religion should be ensured.

(19) Communication should be allowed between persons belonging to national minorities without interference by public authorities and regardless of frontiers; there should be non-discrimination in access to the media.

(20) States will refrain from resettling and condemn all attempts, by the threat or use of force, to resettle persons with the aim of changing the ethnic composition of areas within their territories.

(21) There should be recognition of the particular problems of Roma, including effective measures to achieve full equality of opportunity for them.

(22) Issues concerning national minorities are matters of legitimate international concern and do not exclusively constitute an internal affair of the state in question.

(23) The use of CSCE mechanisms and procedures should contribute to the further protection and promotion of the rights of persons belonging to national minorities.

CSCE principles are, of course, political commitments: they are not legally binding. The *acquis* on minorities represents, nevertheless, the most comprehensive statement of international commitments. All 53 participating states are bound by it[3] and are accountable to their fellow states and to their own citizens in respect of it.

The limits of what can be achieved by way of setting standards have, almost certainly, now been reached. This is due in part to the continuing philosophical divide between states which put the accent on non-discrimination and individual rights, and others which also emphasize group rights and participation.

Implementation

The CSCE has developed four means of encouraging observance of these principles: periodic review of states' adherence to their obligations under the human dimension of the CSCE, including their behaviour towards minorities; the human dimension mechanism – an intergovernmental complaints procedure; the High Commissioner on National Minorities; and ad hoc responses to particular crises involving minorities.

Implementation review

This was a major feature of the CSCE during the Cold War. States outside the Soviet bloc used the follow-up meetings to raise particular issues and to press for improved behaviour – not that treatment of minorities featured largely in the process. Since the end of communism, the emerging democracies have usually been given the benefit of the doubt, and there has been little public criticism. Other countries have been off limits for particular reasons: the West has needed Turkey's cooperation and has sought to advance the cause of human rights through private encouragement rather than public criticism. The Irish and US governments, too, have pursued their interests in Northern Ireland bilaterally rather than through the CSCE.

This trend may be changing: at the Helsinki follow-up meeting there were calls for a more intensive review of states' performance, and for less effort to be spent on the formulation (or re-formulation) of standards. The meeting provided for annual implementation review meetings, the first of which took place in Warsaw in September 1993. This meeting led to criticisms of the performance of a number of states, and at its Rome Council in December 1993 the CSCE asked its Committee of Senior Officials (CSO) and its Permanent Committee to follow these up.

The human dimension mechanism

This has been used over 100 times, mainly in 1989 and 1990. For example, Hungary invoked the mechanism against Romania in respect of the position of the Hungarian minority in Transylvania. Even though the momentum behind use of the procedure has now been lost, it may be used again in the future in the absence of any other interstate complaints procedure. The Rome Council (December 1993) agreed to streamline the mechanism and promote its use. But the evidence, such as it is, suggests that states are less interested in pursuing it than they might be, perhaps while they wait to see how the activities of the High Commissioner on National Minorities develop.

The High Commissioner on National Minorities

Max van der Stoel, the former Foreign Minister of the Netherlands, took up this appointment in January 1993. Acting under the aegis of the Committee of Senior Officials, his task is the prevention of conflict at the earliest possible stage 'in regard to tensions involving national minority issues which have not yet developed beyond an early warning stage, but, in the judgement of the High Commissioner, have the potential to develop into a conflict within the CSCE area affecting peace, stability or relations between participating states ...'. The objective is to direct international attention to future Yugoslavias and Nagorno-Karabakhs. It remains to be seen how inhibiting in practice a clause inserted by Turkey will be, whereby the High Commissioner will not consider national minority issues in situations involving organized acts of terrorism. Another exclusion covers violations of CSCE commitments with regard to individuals. The mandate also lays down procedures for the High Commissioner to collect and receive information, to visit participating states, and to issue early warning of potential conflict (to be communicated by the Chairman in Office to the Committee of Senior Officials). If the High Commissioner believes that further contact and closer consultations will be helpful in achieving solutions, he may make recommendations accordingly to the CSO.

During his first two months in office, he visited the Baltic states and Slovakia. His reports are currently being considered by the parties involved who have the right to comment before they are made known to other participating states. Based in the Hague, he has a small professional staff and a budget for consultants to provide expert advice. He can deal directly with all parties involved. The text lays down simple procedures for communications: the only significant exclusion is communications from any person or organization which practises or publicly condones terrorism or violence. When he is visiting a state, he may hear from governments, local authorities and duly authorized representatives of national minorities.

Two examples of the High Commissioner's work can be cited. In Estonia, the proposed introduction of the new Law on Aliens in June–July 1993 inflamed opinions among the Russian-speaking community. President Yeltsin and other leading Russian politicians spoke rhetorically against the proposed law. After an intervention by Max van der Stoel, President Meri of Estonia agreed to modify the proposed law and opened round-table talks with the Russian community. Max van der Stoel also intervened with positive effect in the disagreement between Albania and Greece in 1993 over the Greek minority in Albania.

The advantages of the High Commissioner's operation are that he can operate swiftly and confidentially anywhere in the CSCE within his mandate. If participating states will not let him enter or travel freely, the matter is to be discussed by the CSO. This is a long-term exercise, and only time will tell to what extent the considerable potential of the office will be realized.

Crises

The CSCE sent its first fact-finding mission to an area of conflict in February 1992 – to Nagorno-Karabakh, Armenia and Azerbaijan. Since then, it has become deeply involved in trying to broker a cease-fire and a long-term solution to the dispute. It has also sent resident missions to Georgia, Estonia, Kosovo, Latvia, Macedonia, Moldova, Sandjak, Tajikistan and Vojvodina. An example of the terms of reference of a CSCE mission is at Annex 2. Common threads are to foster improved relations between communities by mediating in local difficulties and by making known the facts of particular incidents; to help negotiate political solutions (Moldova and Georgia); to be the eyes and ears of the international community; and to contribute to efforts designed to prevent the spread of fighting. As John Major put it at the Helsinki summit, 'The CSCE should not be a watching bystander, a hand-wringing onlooker of Europe's quarrels. The CSCE must develop the means and the will to act before fighting begins.'

It is, of course, early days for these missions, and the problems themselves are among the most difficult in Europe. The missions to Kosovo, Sandjak, and Vojvodina were expelled in July 1993. The CSCE has not always been quick off the mark and this has led to criticism from some intended beneficiaries. There has also been some duplication with UN activities. But at least the CSCE is trying; it has learned the lesson of its own failure and that of other international organizations to grapple with the problems of Yugoslavia at an early stage.

The future

It is clear that the CSCE will not take action in four specific areas. First, it will not agree to prescribe a single set of policies on the form of government for minorities as a panacea. It will recognize the diversity of situations and the need to treat each one on its merits and to find the solution which fits and which can be negotiated. It is not in the business of promoting a regime for minorities based on a supposed group right to self-

determination or autonomy, whether cultural or territorial. But it should respect the right of individual groups and states to advocate solutions based on a form of autonomy and it is likely to find itself promoting regional devolution or autonomy as a basis for settlements where appropriate, as in Nagorno-Karabakh, South Ossetia and Transdniestria.

One strong reason for the CSCE's avoidance of prescription on constitutional questions is that participating states will not surrender their right to decide between the range of policies open to them, which include integration and pluralism. Nearly all fear separatist tendencies and – to paraphrase Dr Patrick Thornberry in his study for the Minority Rights Group of Minorities and Human Rights Law – the CSCE is not a suicide club for states.

Second, the CSCE will not try to emulate the large-scale cooperation programmes of the Council of Europe. The Office of Democratic Institutions and Human Rights in Warsaw will remain relatively small, though with a variety of tasks ranging from organizing the observation of elections on behalf of the CSCE, through servicing CSCE human rights missions and mechanisms, to the organization of seminars involving all 53 CSCE states.

Third, the CSCE will not seek to establish a judicial or treaty-based system for the protection of members of minorities. It will leave this to the UN Human Rights Committee, which supervises the Covenant on Civil and Political Rights, and to the Commission and Court, which do the same for the European Convention on Human Rights. There are no takers in the CSCE at present for the idea that there should be a treaty-based body which can call states to account for infringements of a body of law on the treatment of minorities.

Fourth, the CSCE will not be endowed with mandatory powers to impose sanctions or take enforcement action, on the lines of Chapter 7 of the UN Charter, in order to help end crises involving minorities. Further, states are too attached to a founding principle of the CSCE – the sovereign equality of states – to wish to move rapidly to a limited membership body, taking decisions by vote, on the lines of a European Security Council. The CSCE will seek, as it did in 1992, to improve decision-making by other means while retaining the consensus principle.

There is still plenty of room for the CSCE to develop within these limitations, while seeking to complement the work of other organizations. With an active and effective Chairman in Office and Secretary General, the CSCE will be engaged in areas and activities where it can link diplomatic activity to agreed standards of behaviour.

The consensus rule is less of a constraint than it seems. Since 1992 there have been two ways in which decisions can be taken without consensus. One, already used in respect of Yugoslavia, provides for 'consensus minus one' in the event of clear, gross and uncorrected violations of relevant CSCE commitments. Such actions are to consist of political declarations or other political steps to apply outside the territory of the state concerned – under the different CSCE mechanisms, of course, states are obliged to accept investigatory or problem-solving missions. The CSCE can also oblige two states in dispute to enter into conciliation. This 'consensus minus two' has yet to be tried.

The CSCE works through persuasion. The process by which decisions are reached is time-consuming, and can still be held hostage to the views of dissenting states. But in the absence of power in international law to force states to act, 'peer pressure' through consensus can be more useful than a voting system. It can induce states to accept courses of action to which they are initially opposed. For example, the consensus principle worked in March 1992 in enabling agreement to be reached on the Minsk process for a settlement in Nagorno-Karabakh. To have given Armenia and Azerbaijan a vote would have prevented even this achievement. Subsequent majority votes against the warring parties for failing to fall in with the proposals would have been brushed aside.

Conclusion

The period of standard-setting is largely over. In responding to the problems of minorities, the CSCE is trying to fill two gaps: scrutiny of the record of states in putting agreed principles into practice; and intervention in areas of tension and conflict within and between states involving minorities.

Success will depend largely on the degree of commitment by states. Commitment will show itself in willingness to adjust domestic law and administrative practice, and in readiness to commit resources in terms of people and money to CSCE activities. The CSCE will have a struggle, like the United Nations, to achieve a degree of loyalty and commitment. It is certainly not automatic, and at present is weak for a variety of reasons:

(1) In the new democracies only lip-service has been paid to commitments entered into, on minorities as well as on other subjects. There is, further, the difficulty of living up to democratic ideals in societies with no democratic tradition and in which politics is personalized and domestic means of resolving disputes are embryonic.

(2) More generally, the habit of constructive public criticism of the policy and behaviour of states has been slow to develop at a time when credit is due for heroic efforts to change economies and societies for the better. It remains to be seen whether the 'implementation reviews' will be a formality or whether they will give rise to a genuine exchange of views on controversial and sensitive issues such as the treatment of minorities.

(3) There is lingering unwillingness to admit external involvement.

(4) States are reluctant to spend even more on international organizations.

(5) It is difficult to find the people to staff CSCE missions.

There are bound to be setbacks. But the CSCE will continue to be a means of achieving international political cooperation. As such it will help to deal with the problems affecting minorities. With Yugoslavia in flames, and the lives of millions ruined, it is hard to be optimistic. But the CSCE should be welcomed and encouraged for the modest beginning it has made. It has picked up speed: to maintain momentum it needs to be seen to have succeeded – or at least to have made a difference – in the territories in which it has chosen to involve itself.

Notes

1 What follows is not an authoritative text, but a condensation for descriptive purposes. The full references are: CSCE Final Act, Cmnd 6198, August 1975; Document of the Copenhagen Meeting of the Conference on the Human Dimension of the CSCE, CM1324, November 1990; Document of the Moscow Meeting of the Conference on the Human Dimension of the CSCE, CM 1771, December 1991; Report of the CSCE meeting of experts on National Minorities, Geneva 1991; Charter of Paris for a New Europe CM 1464, March 1991; CSCE Helsinki Document 1992, *The Challenges of Change*, CM 2092, November 1992.

2 Like other international bodies, the CSCE has not laid down a definition of minorities. The term is taken to refer to non-dominant groups in a numerical minority in a state. 'National' refers to nationality of the state in order to distinguish the people concerned from non-national groups such as migrants.

3 Turkey has entered a reservation that as far as it is concerned national minorities are only those that are recognized in an international treaty.

Annex 1: Extract from report of Geneva experts meeting on national minorities

Aware of the diversity and varying constitutional systems among them, which make no single approach necessarily generally applicable, the participating States note with interest that positive results have been obtained by some of them in an appropriate democratic manner by, *inter alia*:

- Advisory and decision-making bodies in which minorities are represented, in particular with regard to education, culture and religion;
- Elected bodies and assemblies of national minority affairs;
- Local and autonomous administration, as well as autonomy on a territorial basis, including the existence of consultative, legislative and executive bodies chosen through free and periodic elections;
- Self-administration by a national minority of aspects concerning its identity in situations where autonomy on a territorial basis does not apply;
- Decentralized or local forms of government;
- Bilateral and multilateral agreements and other arrangements regarding national minorities;
- For persons belonging to national minorities, provision of adequate types and levels of education in their mother tongue with due regard to the number, geographic settlement patterns and cultural traditions of national minorities;
- Funding the teaching of minority languages to the general public, as well as the inclusion of minority languages in teacher-training institutions, in particular in regions inhabited by persons belonging to national minorities;
- In cases where instruction in a particular subject is not provided in their territory in the minority language at all levels, taking the necessary measures to find means of recognising diplomas issued abroad for a course of study completed in that language;
- Creation of government research agencies to review legislation and disseminate information related to equal rights and non-discrimination;
- Provision of financial and technical assistance to persons belonging to national minorities who so wish to exercise their right to establish and maintain their own educational, cultural and religious institutions, organisations and associations;

- Governmental assistance for addressing local difficulties relating to discriminatory practices (e.g. a citizens relations service);
- Encouragement of grassroots community relations efforts between minority communities, between majority and minority communities, and between neighbouring communities sharing borders, aimed at helping to prevent local tensions from arising and [to] address conflicts peacefully should they arise; and
- Encouragement of the establishment of permanent mixed commissions, either inter-State or regional, to facilitate continuing dialogue between the border regions concerned.

The participating States are of the view that these or other approaches, individually or in combination, could be helpful in improving the situation of national minorities on their territories.

Annex 2: CSCE Mission to the Republic of Moldova

Objective of the Mission
The objective of the Mission is to facilitate the achievement of a lasting comprehensive political settlement, on the basis of CSCE principles and commitments, of the conflict in the Left-Bank Dniester areas of the Republic of Moldova in all its aspects.

Mission activities
To this end the Mission will:

- Facilitate the establishment of a comprehensive political framework for dialogue and negotiations and assist the parties to the conflict in pursuing negotiations on a lasting political settlement of the conflict, consolidating the independence and sovereignty of the Republic of Moldova along with an understanding about a special status for the Trans-Dniester region;
- Gather and provide information on the situation, including the military situation, in the region, investigate specific incidents and assess their political implications;
- Encourage the participating states concerned in pursuing negotiations on an agreement on the status and the early, orderly and complete withdrawal of foreign troops;
- Provide advice and expertise, as well as a framework for other

contributions, on such parts of a political settlement as effective observance of international obligations and commitments regarding human and minority rights, democratic transformation, repatriation of refugees, definition of a special status of the Trans-Dniester region;
- Initiate a visible CSCE presence in the region and establish contacts with all parties to the conflict, local authorities and local populations.

Mission area
The Mission will establish offices in Bendery and/or Tiraspol and operate predominantly in the Left-Bank Dniester areas of the Republic of Moldova, with headquarters established in Chisinau.

Cooperation and coordination
Pursuant to information received by the Chairman in Office and upon her direction the Head of Mission will establish appropriate contacts with representatives of the United Nations and other international organisations with an active interest in contributing to the resolution of the conflict, on coordination and cooperation with the Mission.

The Mission will cooperate and liaise with representatives of the existing trilateral and quadripartite mechanisms established to deal with the conflict.

Size and composition
The Mission will be composed initially of 8 members, taking into account the need for administrative and other experts. The Head of Mission will be appointed by the Chairman in Office. The other members of the Mission will be appointed by the Head of Mission. All participating States are eligible to participate in the Mission.

10

CONCLUSIONS

HUGH MIALL

As the contributors to this volume suggest, the present transnational regime for protecting minority rights is unsatisfactory. European states are signatories to agreements which commit them to allow persons belonging to national minorities to 'exercise fully and effectively their human rights and fundamental freedoms without any discrimination and in full equality before the law'.[1] Yet minorities in many states suffer discrimination, and the human rights of persons belonging to them are abused. In extreme cases, the lack of adequate protection, either in domestic law or by transnational means, acts as an incentive for national minorities to claim their own states. Peaceful secession is not unknown, but more often such claims lead to civil conflict and war.

The difficulties of minorities are linked to the nature of international society. In a system of nation-states in which the majority nation holds power, minorities can be in an unenviable situation. While some European borders do accurately reflect the distribution of peoples, many others are arbitrary lines which cut across peoples, the outcomes of past wars or former administrative boundaries. But even if a benevolent being had designed them carefully, no European borders could avoid creating large numbers of minorities, unless Europe were to become even more of a mosaic than the Holy Roman Empire was in the sixteenth and seventeenth centuries. Such fragmentation would not be desirable for international society; nor would it accord with the view, accepted by CSCE members, that minorities are a permanent feature of states and a source of enrichment for European society. Minorities and states must therefore be made compatible with one another. In the Cold War, this was done by suppressing minorities. If post-Cold War Europe is to fulfil democratic

112

aspirations, it will have to find ways to make states more friendly to minorities.

Adjustments in the political and legal order

In Chapter 2, James Mayall refers to Hedley Bull's conception of a 'new medievalism'. This is a new form of international society in which the jurisdictional monopoly of states is broken and other forms of overlapping authority are accepted. In some respects, west European institutions and the CSCE are already moving in this direction. The Council of Europe enables individuals and organizations to appeal to the European Court of Justice. CSCE member states have agreed that 'commitments undertaken in the field of the human dimension of the CSCE are matters of direct and legitimate concern to all participating states and do not belong exclusively to the internal affairs of the state concerned'.[2] These are first steps towards developing an international civil society, in which human rights and the legal protection of people complement the rights of states.

Other recently published studies of the problems of minorities point in a similar direction. Gidon Gottlieb, in his study for the Council on Foreign Relations, *Nation Against State*, argues that 'the international legal community can be broadened beyond states and international organizations to formally include peoples and nations. Nations and peoples that have no state of their own can be recognized as such and endowed with an international legal status.' Such a measure, he argues, need not compromise the territorial integrity of states, but recognizes the overlapping nature of peoples, states and legal authorities in a complex world society.[3]

In some degree national minorities already have recently established rights which go in this direction. These are stated in the UN Declaration on the Rights of Persons belonging to National or Ethnic, Religious and Linguistic Minorities, which Patrick Thornberry summarizes in Chapter 3, and they are echoed in the Concluding Document of the Copenhagen CSCE Meeting (Chapter IV, Article 32):

> Persons belonging to national minorities have the right freely to express, preserve and develop their ethnic, cultural, linguistic, or religious identity and to maintain and develop their culture in all its aspects, free of any attempt at assimilation against their will. In particular, they have the right ... to establish and maintain

113

unimpeded contacts among themselves within their country as well as contacts across frontiers with citizens of other States with whom they share a common ethnic or national origin, cultural heritage or religious beliefs; ... [and] to establish and maintain organizations or associations within their country and to participate in international non-governmental organizations. Persons belonging to national minorities can exercise their rights individually as well as in community with other members of their group.

Such declarations offer a glimpse of the 'architecture of [an] eventual regime for minorities', to which Patrick Thornberry refers in Chapter 3. There is still room, as he shows, for further development and consolidation of minority rights in law, despite the recent progress. One can identify as weaknesses in the current legal regime, first, the lack of a satisfactory definition of minorities and the uncertainty over whether minority rights are restricted to nationals of the states in which they dwell; second, the lack of a right to some form of 'self-management': this can be remedied by strengthening the participation rights of minority groups; and, third, the weakness of collective rights relative to the rights of persons. The work of standard-setting and legislation is certainly not over yet.

The major obstacle to minority protection, however, lies in the inadequate implementation of existing rights. It is easy to point to cases where states harass minority organizations and prevent transnational contacts across borders. States and international organizations have a duty to uphold the rights agreed at the UN and at Moscow in their own territories and against delinquent states. The following sections discuss domestic means to fulfil these obligations and transnational responses.

Measures within states

The present legal order places the main burden for protecting minority rights on measures within the state. The obligation not to discriminate against persons belonging to minorities and to respect their identity is crucial. In order to reach a workable political accommodation between minority and majority communities, measures for effective political participation are usually the key issue.

In his recent discussion paper, Kamal Shehadi argues that there needs to be a bargain between states and minorities, to reduce the risks and increase the benefits of living together.[4] This implies making special

political arrangements for minorities. Asbjørn Eide, in another recent study, distinguishes between the 'common domain', in which the same rights should apply to all citizens, and the 'separate domain', in which special measures to protect the identity of the minority are justified.[5] In the 'common domain', states are obliged to uphold all relevant international standards. But measures in the 'separate domain' may also be necessary, for example to guarantee the development of cultural expression and education in the minority's language and to provide for minority self-administration in policy areas affecting its special interests. The South Tyrol case (Chapter 5) is clearly one in which a 'separate domain' has evolved over time, in a way that has not posed a threat to the territorial integrity of the state concerned.

In considering political arrangements within the state, it is necessary to be sensitive to the diversity of ethnographic and political conditions. Minority situations vary, depending on the size, nature and dispersion of the minority and on the political culture of the majority community. Certain measures may be appropriate where the minority forms only 5 or 10 per cent of the population, and different measures where it forms 40 or 50 per cent. The seriousness of the situation may range from, for example, inadequate provision for native language in schools, to threats to the very survival of the minority. In some societies a full democratic system is operating, in others the preconditions for minority protection are scarcely in place.

It is possible to identify a range of general measures to assist minorities, many of which are in force in European states. Protection of minority languages, provision of education in minority languages, the right of the minority to its own media and to have access to publicly controlled media, participation in advisory and decision-making bodies, national representation, and economic and social protection (including affirmative action if necessary to redress inequalities) are among them. Eide offers a comprehensive list.[6]

But political arrangements depend on the circumstances. Where minorities can exercise some form of self-governance, potential tensions between the minority and the state are often defused (though, as Antony Alcock points out in Chapter 5, continuous adjustment is needed). The development in Spain of regional autonomy, within the framework of the 1978 constitution, took much of the heat out of Basque and Catalan separatism. The Belgian constitution of 1971 gave considerable autonomy to linguistic areas, enabling a bi-national society to live together without violent conflict. The Swiss system of cantons is another well-

known model of successful multinational government. It is possible to satisfy demands for self-determination in ways which fall short of the creation of new states. Autonomy and other forms of self-governance are means whereby states and minorities can strike a bargain which need not be to the disadvantage of either side. This is not to argue that autonomy is appropriate in every case: in Northern Ireland the challenge is to find an agreed framework of political arrangements in the 'common domain' which provides for the full political participation of both communities.

In order to preserve equality, it is essential that persons belonging to minorities have full citizenship rights in the states in which they dwell. A number of new states in central and eastern Europe have established an ethnic, or partly ethnic, qualification for citizenship. Such restrictions should be challenged on the basis of international agreements, and existing members of the EU and the Council of Europe should take steps to remove ethnic criteria from their citizenship laws.

Measures to redress the balance between minorities and states will naturally be difficult to carry out in practice, especially in post-communist societies and in societies which lack democracy. In a climate of rampant nationalism, and in nations which bear historical grievances against their neighbours, it is understandable that a spirit of compromise and pluralism will take time to develop.

The conflict between majorities and minorities has a psychological component. If majorities stigmatize minorities, it is often because the majority feels insecure. A response which seeks to make post-communist societies more secure, while pressing for measures to accommodate minorities, is therefore needed. Support for economic development and democratization are probably preconditions for assisting minorities. Within this broad framework, there are a number of more specific ways in which the international community can seek to promote minority rights.

Transnational measures

There is little doubt that the developing body of international law and European political standards can benefit minority groups. They have made a contribution, for example, to the easing of the conflicts in the Baltic states over citizenship. They provide a yardstick for citizens to hold their own states to account. They also offer a means for states to appraise constitutional practice and domestic legislation. The adoption of minority rights as a criterion that is taken into account by the European Union

in considering membership applications and by international financial institutions in considering loans gives a certain 'bite' to the standards which applicants cannot readily afford to neglect.

The Council of Europe already plays a valuable role in advising states on minority issues and human rights, commenting on laws, and assisting and advising national minorities. The Council of Europe also develops initiatives which address minority issues locally and in regions. Such 'bottom-up' measures are important and could be much expanded. The CSCE High Commissioner for National Minorities also intercedes between states and minorities, and encourages dialogue; his intervention in Estonia was followed by President Meri's decision to set up a forum to promote dialogue between the Estonian and Russian-speaking communities. 'Top-level' agreements such as these often need to be followed up on the ground, for example by providing legal advice centres to inform persons belonging to minorities of their rights. NGOs also have an important role to play through transnational contacts at government and grass-roots levels.

'Euroregions' (Chapter 8) are a valuable innovation which can assist minorities to 'maintain unimpeded contacts ... across frontiers'. The Council of Europe supports them; and there is scope for expansion. If European patterns of jurisdiction are to become richer and overlapping, the regional level of development has an important part to play.

James Mayall (Chapter 2) refers to developing a *droit de regard* to make states accountable to one another. If it became recognized that all European states were open to outside monitoring, minority groups might gain confidence that international institutions were aware of their plight and willing to act. The CSCE implementation review meetings and monitoring missions are important innovations and they should be maintained in the interests of transparency and verification. It is important that Western states set high standards of openness.

Even where minority rights are abused, as in Kosovo, outside observers can have a moderating effect (Chapter 7). CSCE observers and missions have visited many of the potential trouble-spots in Europe. They can alert the CSCE to incipient trouble and foster dialogue at local and intergovernmental levels. The long-term missions and the work of the High Commissioner for National Minorities appear particularly valuable, yet the scale of this preventive diplomacy is small in relation to the magnitude of the problems.

There is a strong argument for applying 'conditionality' on the basis of observance of human rights in loans, aid and institutional contacts.

117

Such conditionality already operates in principle, and could be used more to encourage adherence to international commitments, though it is likely that a balance will need to be drawn between this imperative and the requirement for a flexible policy to encourage stabilization even in states with poor human rights records. Conditions should certainly be applied when states are recognized. The failure of the EC to take note of its own Badinter Commission's recommendations on Croatia's inadequate minority guarantees sent a particularly unfortunate signal, which was reinforced by the EC conference's subsequent acceptance of the plan for cantonization of Bosnia on ethnic grounds.

Despite these precedents, enlargement of European institutions (especially the Council of Europe and the European Union) can be expected to improve the position of minorities in the long run. As the Northern Ireland case shows, such improvement is not automatic; but the Anglo-Irish agreement and the growth in cross-border cooperation owed much to talks in the margin of European Council meetings. Ethnic Hungarians in Slovakia might feel more secure in a European Union that contained both Slovakia and Hungary. This is not to deny that enlargement faces its own pitfalls and difficulties.

Border changes

The international community is rightly nervous of changing borders. If internationally agreed borders were treated lightly, competition for territory could become a free-for-all. However, CSCE principles allow for changes by agreement. Where borders, especially formerly internal administrative borders, cut across peoples unnecessarily, and where communities within the same borders cannot live together, agreed border changes are justified. Similarly, peacefully negotiated secession is justified when majority–minority relations have broken down. The EU Stability Pact conference, which the French government proposed should start in 1994, is planned to address borders and minority guarantees together. If it can find common ground, this will be a valuable initiative.

Intervention

Where civil order has broken down altogether, protection of minorities is the first casualty. Some argue that the international community is justified in intervening to redress massive breaches of human rights. Others caution that intervention endangers the principles of state sovereignty

and territorial integrity on which international order depends. The present legal and political order, as reflected in Article 2(7) of the UN Charter and in the 1975 Helsinki Principles of the CSCE, gives more support to the second position. Nevertheless, principle and practice have been shifting since the end of the Cold War. As mentioned above, European states have agreed that their human dimension commitments are matters of common concern. The cases of the 'no-fly zones' in Iraq and Bosnia-Herzegovina, and the willingness to supply humanitarian relief even when the host state is uncooperative, are signs of the change. The UN Security Council can act to assist civil populations under Chapter 7 of the Charter, if it so chooses. As the international community comes to recognize the rights of people as well as states, international intervention to assist people is likely to become accepted as legitimate. James Mayall (Chapter 2) argues that it would be in keeping with the development of an international civil society to develop a capacity to intervene to prevent massive abuse of human rights (though he recognizes that in the short term China and other states would block a Charter reform in this direction).

The form that such intervention should take is another matter. Some argue that, where there is a just cause and legal authority and other means have been exhausted, the international community must be prepared to use force. Gottlieb argues for continuous air attacks aimed at toppling the governments of oppressive states.[7] However, one may be sceptical of whether such attacks would benefit the minorities concerned. Direct assistance to minorities and non-military sanctions are other options.

Minority rights: a European responsibility

The present situation of minorities in many parts of Europe is bleak. The appalling practice of 'ethnic cleansing' has opened a chapter of forced population movements which starkly illustrates one alternative to a civilized regime for minority rights. In politically unstable and economically insecure societies, where exclusive nationalism gets a ready hearing, the vulnerability of minorities is evident.

Nevertheless, there have been positive steps in recent years to develop the beginnings of a transnational regime to protect minority rights. It is all the more urgent now to consolidate and strengthen it. While for the time being the main burden of adjustment will have to lie with measures within the state, stronger transnational measures are necessary to encourage such adjustment. Developing a stronger regime for minority rights is

possible if Europeans are serious about supporting democratic consolidation within their own states and across European frontiers.

Notes

1 *Document of the Copenhagen Meeting of the CSCE Conference on the Human Dimension*, 1990.
2 *Preamble to the Document of the Moscow Meeting of the Conference on the Human Dimension of the CSCE*, October 1991.
3 Gidon Gottlieb, *Nation Against State: A New Approach to Ethnic Conflicts and the Decline of Sovereignty* (New York: Council on Foreign Relations, 1993), p. 39.
4 Kamal S. Shehadi, *Ethnic Self-Determination and the Break-up of States*, Adelphi Paper No. 238 (London: International Institute of Strategic Studies, December 1993), p. 59.
5 Asbjørn Eide, *New Approaches to Minority Protection* (London: Minority Rights Group, December 1993).
6 Asbjørn Eide, 'Recommendations to the UN-Subcommission on the protection of minorities', in Eide, op. cit.
7 Gottlieb, op. cit., p. 119.

The Council on Foreign Relations publishes authoritative and timely books on international affairs and American foreign policy. Designed for the interested citizen and specialist alike, the Council's rich assortment of studies covers topics ranging from economics to regional conflict to U.S.–Soviet relations. If you would like more information, please write:

Council on Foreign Relations Press
58 East 68th Street
New York, NY 10021
Telephone: (212) 734-0400
FAX: (212) 861-2759

MINORITY RIGHTS
IN EUROPE